Happily Homemade

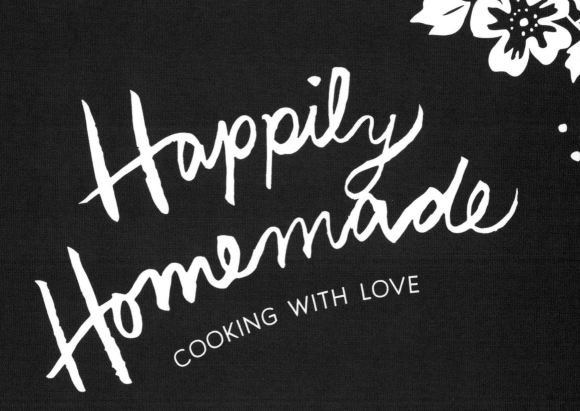

Happily Homemade

COOKING WITH LOVE

RACHEL SCHULTZ

ZONDERVAN®

ZONDERVAN

Happily Homemade

Copyright © 2017 by Rachel Schultz

Requests for information should be addressed to:

Zondervan, 3900 Sparks Dr., SE, Grand Rapids, MI 49546

ISBN 978-0-310-35712-4

Published in association with the literary agency of Wolgemuth & Associates, Inc.

Cover design: Milkglass Creative, LLC

Cover and interior photography: Rachel Schultz

Interior illustration: Milkglass Creative, LLC

Interior design: Lori Lynch

Printed in China

17 18 19 20 21 22 23 24 / DSC / 22 21 20 19 18 17 16 15 14 13 12 11 10 9 8 7 6 5 4 3 2 1

TO DAVID LEE SCHULTZ

CONTENTS

WELCOME TO MY KITCHEN

What is my kitchen like? There is probably a pile of fruits and vegetables on the counter in the process of being peeled and sliced to have ready for later. Nearby on the ground you might see a half-eaten cookie abandoned near a collection of toys. There is a calendar on the wall with birthdays and anniversaries of the friends who frequent our table. I can usually get my kitchen clean once in the morning, and the rest of the day is more or less spent trying to get it back that way again (especially with crumbs where a certain little guy sits). My days are spent as wife to David and mother of two babies. I savor the early part of each evening when I can cook up something warm and nourishing to put on the table for the ones I love.

In the following pages, I want to focus on the best use of your time in the kitchen, even if that time is limited. *Homemade* does not have to also mean *dreaded* or *slaved over*. (We crave a boxed mix of muffins now and then too.) I particularly do not want to have you go through the rigor of making a complicated meal only to end up thinking the canned beef ravioli might have been a better choice. (I have been there. Terrible!) As simple as it sounds, I hope to help you master the things you have to do in the kitchen every day—especially things that make life nicer for you and your family.

How is this possible? For me, the two keys are practice (lots of it!) and help from others. For that reason, a few of my dearest friends have agreed to share their best tips in some special features peppered throughout this book. Whether your kitchen and family are like mine, or even if you are quite different, you can bring warmth and delight to everyone at your table when you serve something happily homemade.

MY FAVORITE TOOLS

Food processor: I use this all the time to help prep work go faster or to make easy sauces and dressings.

Funnel: The night I came home from the store all excited about our new (4-inch diameter) funnel, David was amused and a little confused. But once you have a funnel, you will find it incredibly useful for pouring liquids, grains, spices, and more—without the mess.

Garlic press: Fresh garlic is a must, and a garlic press makes working with tiny cloves easier.

Glass 9 x 13-inch baking pans: I purchased ones that come with rubber lids, which are so useful when transporting or refrigerating food.

Good, sharp knives: After badly cutting myself with a too-dull knife, I learned the time and money spent on having good-quality knives professionally sharpened is worth it. My chef's knife is never far from me when I am cooking.

Mini colander: I use this several times a week, especially when working with beans. A tiny (6-inch) one is much less cumbersome than dragging out your big pasta strainer.

Nonstick frying pans and skillets: When we first got married, I tried the high-maintenance stainless steel pans and promptly returned them. I was relieved to have a high-quality nonstick set instead.

Pastry cutter: This little device is useful for many tasks beyond its job description, such as mashing bananas or avocado.

Rice cooker: Really fluffy and soft rice is kind of my favorite thing ever. One of these is a smart investment.

Rimmed baking sheets: I use these every day and for many different things. Plus, it is so satisfying to have a matching set that stack perfectly onto each other.

Rubber spatula: This is my utensil of choice. I use it for far more things than it is probably intended for, and it never disappoints.

Stand mixer: Everyone loves hands-free mixing and achieving that perfectly uniform batter.

Waterproof oven mitt: You will never burn your hands straining boiling water again.

MY FAVORITE INGREDIENTS

Butter: Always the real stuff!

Garlic: I know it is less convenient, but seriously, use fresh whenever you can. It is worth it.

Ghee, or clarified butter: Think of it like a more intense butter, great for sautéing.

Hard-boiled eggs: These are a healthy snack for kids, but they also are a nice topper for salads and many breakfasts. We always have a few ready in the refrigerator. I make them by placing the eggs in the base of a saucepan and covering them with a few inches of water. Then, I bring the water to a boil over high heat, remove the saucepan from the heat, and let it sit for 10 minutes before straining.

Maple syrup: Like true Michiganders, we love this stuff. Try using it just about anytime you would normally use honey.

Mustard powder: A lesser-known spice that is fabulous for flavor. (Put it in your burgers!)

Oil and vinegar: The classic dressing that cannot be beat. Sometimes I even skip the oil and have just balsamic vinegar on my salad.

Raw turbinado sugar: My preferred sugar for topping desserts and baked goods.

Sliced almonds: We often end up tossing these on everything from appetizers to desserts. They are our favorite way to add a healthy crunch.

Sweet Vidalia onions: Almost always the onion I use.

Vegetable broth: I like to keep this on hand and never bother with chicken or beef broth, because it works for everything (chicken, beef, vegetables, whatever). Plus, it is easier to make yourself—no raw meat handling necessary.

Whole milk: A must for baking! When following recipes that call for water, I like to experiment with using milk instead for a creamier taste.

KITCHEN TIPS AND CHARTS

- Leave vegetables in large pieces when putting them into a slow cooker to help keep their shape and individual flavor.

- To save time on baking potatoes but still have great texture, microwave them for 2 minutes on high before roasting.

- Keep knives sharp longer by using the blunt side to scrape ingredients from the cutting board.

- Meal plan! Meal plan! Meal plan! This is my best tip for saving time and money. See page 84 for more details on how I do this.

- Quickly shred cooked chicken by using a hand mixer (either the beaters or the hooks work).

- Perfectly ripened-for-baking bananas can be frozen to thaw and use later.

- My favorite way to prepare four boneless chicken breasts is to drizzle them with olive oil, then season with salt and pepper. Roast for 40 minutes at 425 degrees, flipping halfway.

- When baking, experiment with making the final product more moist by substituting half of the white sugar with brown sugar.

- Keep a designated open box of baking soda in the refrigerator to absorb odors.

- Toss lemon and lime peels in the garbage disposal instead of throwing them away. They will help clear debris and create a fresh scent.

MEAT DONENESS TEMPERATURES

Medium-rare beef	135°F
Fish	140°F
Medium beef, medium-rare pork	145°F
Medium pork	150°F
Well-done beef	155°F
Well-done pork	160°F
Ground meat and poultry	170°F

OVEN TEMPERATURE CONVERSIONS

250°F / 120°C	very low
300°F / 150°C	low
325°F / 170°C	warm
350°F / 180°C	moderate
375°F / 190°C	moderately hot
400°F / 200°C	moderately hotter
425°F / 220°C	hot
450°F / 230°C	extremely hot

MEASUREMENT CONVERSIONS

1/2 tablespoon = 1 1/2 teaspoons

1 tablespoon = 3 teaspoons

2 tablespoons = 1 ounce

4 tablespoons = 1/4 cup = 2 ounces

8 tablespoons = 1/2 cup = 4 ounces

10 tablespoons + 2 teaspoons = 2/3 cup

1 cup = 1/2 pint = 8 ounces

2 cups = 1 pint = 16 ounces

2 pints = 1 quart = 32 ounces

4 quarts = 1 gallon = 128 ounces

METRIC VOLUME CONVERSIONS

1/8 teaspoon = .5 ml

1/4 teaspoon = 1.23 ml

1/2 teaspoon = 2.5 ml

1 teaspoon = 15 ml

2 tablespoons (1 ounce) = 30 ml

1/4 cup (2 ounces) = 60 ml

1/3 cup (2.67 ounces) = 75 ml

1/2 cup (4 ounces) = 120 ml

3/4 cup (6 ounces) = 180 ml

1 cup (8 ounces) = 240 ml

METRIC WEIGHT CONVERSIONS

1/2 ounce = 14 grams

1 ounce = 29 grams

1 1/2 ounces = 43 grams

2 ounces = 57 grams

4 ounces = 227 grams

16 ounces (1 pound) = 454 grams

HALVING RECIPES

1 cup to $^1/_2$ cup

$^3/_4$ cup to 6 tablespoons

$^2/_3$ cup to $^1/_3$ cup

$^1/_2$ cup to $^1/_4$ cup

$^1/_3$ cup to 2 tablespoons + 2 teaspoons

$^1/_4$ cup to 2 tablespoons

1 tablespoon to 1 $^1/_2$ teaspoons

1 teaspoon to $^1/_2$ teaspoon

$^1/_2$ teaspoon to $^1/_4$ teaspoons

BAKING SUBSTITUTIONS

1 banana = 2 eggs

$^1/_2$ cup applesauce = 2 eggs

3 tablespoons peanut butter = 1 egg

1 cup applesauce = 1 cup butter

1 avocado = $^1/_2$ cup butter

1 cup applesauce = 1 cup oil

$^3/_4$ cup honey = 1 cup sugar

$^1/_2$ teaspoon cream of tartar + $^1/_4$ teaspoon baking soda = 1 teaspoon baking powder

1 cup buttermilk = 1 cup yogurt

1 tablespoon corn starch = 2 tablespoons flour

1 teaspoon lemon juice = $^1/_2$ teaspoon apple cider vinegar

1 tablespoon mustard = $^1/_2$ teaspoon ground mustard

1 cup sugar = 2 cups powdered sugar

PRODUCE STORAGE

Apple: at room temperature until ripe, or in the refrigerator up to 1 month

Asparagus: in the refrigerator up to 1 week

Avocado: at room temperature until ripe, or in the refrigerator up to 5 days

Banana: at room temperature until ripe, or in the refrigerator up to 5 days

Bell pepper: in the refrigerator up to 2 weeks

Berry: in the refrigerator up to 1 week

Broccoli: in the refrigerator up to 1 week

Brussels sprout: in the refrigerator up to 1 week

Cabbage: in the refrigerator up to 1 week

Carrot: in the refrigerator up to 3 weeks

Cauliflower: in the refrigerator up to 1 week

Celery: in the refrigerator up to 2 weeks

Cucumber: in the refrigerator up to 1 week

Garlic: at room temperature up to 3 weeks

Grape: at room temperature until ripe, or in the refrigerator up to 1 week

Green bean: at room temperature until ripe, or in the refrigerator up to 1 week

Kale: in the refrigerator up to 1 week

Kiwi: at room temperature until ripe, or in the refrigerator up to 1 week

Lemon: in the refrigerator up to 2 weeks

Lime: in the refrigerator up to 2 weeks

Mango: at room temperature until ripe, or in the refrigerator up to 1 week

Mushroom: in the refrigerator up to 1 week

Onion, green: in the refrigerator up to 2 weeks

Onion, whole: at room temperature up to 3 weeks, or in the refrigerator up to 2 months

Onion, sliced: in the refrigerator up to 1 week

Potato: at room temperature up to 2 weeks

Spinach: in the refrigerator up to 1 week

Tomato: at room temperature up to 1 week

MENU IDEAS

Brunch
White Chocolate French Toast Kabobs, Maple Sweet Potato Hash Browns, and Cream Cheese Tart

Christmas Morning
Niki's Dark Chocolate Scones and Three Cheese Omelets

Snacks for the Big Game
Avocado Deviled Eggs, Loaded Skillet Fries, and Raspberry Roasted Cheese Dip

Afternoon Treat
Chocolate and Cranberry Breakfast Cookies and Doughnut Milkshake

Fancy Dinner
Sweet Potato and Roasted Grape Crostini, Beet and Kale Lasagna Roll-Ups, and Coconut Macaroons

Children's Sleepover
BBQ Chicken Pizza Bread, Coconut Almond Chocolate Popcorn, and S'more Cupcakes

Summer Cookout
Brad's Spatchcock Chicken, Watermelon and Pistachio Salad, and Strawberry Lemon Sorbet

BREAKFASTS

Spinach and Mushroom Polenta

Cream Cheese Tart

Three Cheese Omelet

Rosemary Grapefruit Puff Pancake

Chocolate and Cranberry Breakfast Cookie

Carissa's German Crepes

Breakfast Pitas

Flourless Yogurt and Banana Pancakes

Breakfast Croissant Sandwich

Blueberry Cheesecake Stuffed French Toast

Niki's Dark Chocolate Scones

Pumpkin and Pecan Baked Oatmeal

Herbed Mini Quiches

White Chocolate French Toast Kabobs

Maple Sweet Potato Hash Browns

I LOVE YOU, EVERY DAY

Most days while I am preparing a meal, I have one of my little ones nearby, stretching out his arms to be held. Sometimes I feel pulled in too many directions, but then I remind myself that the purpose of all this cooking is to pour love into the hearts in my home. Shooing off the children to make a "perfect" meal (or to prepare it in quiet!) means I am probably sabotaging my own efforts. If my aim is to show them love, not treating their needs as annoyances is as much a way to care for them as having food for the table.

I want my family to look back on our years together and be able to say I made our home happy. Maybe they will say I managed to make mealtime fun or that I helped everyone feel welcomed and loved. Or maybe they will think I at least was marked by gentleness while trying! Hopefully this gentleness will come in important parenting moments when I extend grace and teach wisdom. But I wonder if most of my gentleness will be shown in everyday moments, like when I make sure my toddler's bathwater is the right temperature, or when I bundle the babies up so they will stay perfectly warm outside, or when I might lean over to my daughter at dinner to whisper I had her in mind when I decided to make those favorite mashed potatoes sitting on the table.

This is all part of the endeavor to be a wife, a mother, and a woman who nourishes her little community. We bring light. We work to overlook mistakes and interruptions and inconveniences. We provide for needs and (some) wants. We choose not to think of impressing all the people out there, but to find more value in being hardworking for and compassionate to our handful of people in here.

I see sharing food as an important way to do this (we eat multiple times a day, after all). I can figure out how to save on groceries so I can buy the granola bars my husband likes and hide them in his gym bag. I can make sure dinner is warm and ready when he gets home, since he is always hungry that time of day. I can carefully feed my daughter her bottle. I can put together a nutritious breakfast for my son so he feels healthy and strong, and also let him join me in taste testing the chocolate chips. I can let the children help with the big people stuff in the kitchen, even when it takes longer and gets messier. And whether our time at the table is a long, leisurely affair or a bit rushed, I hope they will see every meal, along with so many other everyday moments, is one more drop in the bucket of me saying, *Hey, I love you.*

SPINACH AND MUSHROOM POLENTA

Polenta is a neat ingredient to experiment with (and it can be found in your local grocery store!). This savory dish almost demands to be eaten while cuddled up in a blanket on a blustery day, but I think it is delicious any time of year.

Serves 2

2 cups vegetable broth

1 cup polenta

3 tablespoons butter

5 baby bella mushrooms, sliced

2 cups spinach

1 clove garlic, minced

¼ teaspoon salt

¼ teaspoon black pepper

1 cup ricotta cheese

¼ teaspoon dried parsley

¼ teaspoon dried thyme

¼ cup grated Parmesan cheese

1. Place vegetable broth in a large pot and bring to a boil over high heat. Add polenta and stir. Reduce heat to low and simmer for 40 minutes, stirring frequently.
2. Melt butter in a medium skillet over medium heat and sauté the mushrooms for 5 to 7 minutes. Add spinach and garlic and sauté for 1 to 2 more minutes. Season with salt and pepper. Remove from heat.
3. Stir ricotta into the polenta and add the parsley and thyme.
4. Serve the spinach-and-mushroom mixture over polenta and top with Parmesan.

CREAM CHEESE TART

Frozen puff pastry is a marvelously easy way to enjoy breads and crusts straight from your oven without having to start from scratch. Unlike some of its frozen premade cousins, this tart comes out light and fresh.

Serves 3 to 4

1 (½-pound) puff pastry, thawed

1 (8-ounce) package cream cheese, softened

3 tablespoons milk

½ cup powdered sugar

1 cup seasonal berries

1. Preheat oven to 400 degrees.
2. Roll out puff pastry and transfer dough to a parchment paper–lined baking sheet. Fold in edges about half an inch to form the crust. Use a fork to poke holes into the rest of the dough. Bake for 20 minutes.
3. Beat together cream cheese, milk, and powdered sugar in a stand mixer.
4. Remove pastry from oven and press down center with fork if it has puffed. Allow to cool. Spread cream cheese mixture onto tart. Top with fruit. Slice into rectangles.

THREE CHEESE OMELET

My husband once said, "If a stool requires three legs to stand, why stop at two cheeses for an omelet?" This sound logic led to the creation of this extra-cheesy, flavor-rich version of a staple breakfast item. Indeed, good things often come in threes!

Serves 4

4 large eggs, separated

1/2 teaspoon honey

1 teaspoon half-and-half

1/2 teaspoon salt

1/2 teaspoon black pepper

1/2 tablespoon butter

1/2 cup shredded white Cheddar cheese

1/2 cup shredded Muenster cheese

1/3 cup grated Parmesan, plus extra for garnish

3 green onions, sliced

1. In a medium bowl combine egg yolks, honey, half-and-half, salt, and pepper and whisk together with a fork.
2. In a separate bowl whisk egg whites with an electric mixer on high for 3 to 4 minutes, until soft peaks form.
3. Fold egg whites into egg yolk mixture.
4. Melt butter in a small skillet over medium-low heat.
5. Spread 1/4 of egg mixture evenly into skillet. Sprinkle with white Cheddar, Muenster, and Parmesan.
6. Cook for 3 minutes. Flip and cook other side for 1 to 2 minutes.
7. Fold in half and top with green onions and additional Parmesan, salt, and pepper.
8. Repeat steps 5 through 7 to make three more omelets.

ROSEMARY GRAPEFRUIT
PUFF PANCAKE

This recipe creates a fluffier texture than what you will find in a typical stack of flapjacks, and the flavor combination is very fun. I have a particular aversion to dried rosemary (or should I say "pine needles"?), so I recommend using the fresh stuff for this. You can always substitute other fruits and toppings too.

Serves 1 to 2

½ cup all-purpose flour

½ cup milk

3 tablespoons sugar

Pinch of ground cinnamon

½ teaspoon salt

1 teaspoon vanilla extract

3 large eggs

3 tablespoons butter

1 medium grapefruit, sliced

Fresh rosemary

Powdered sugar

1. Preheat oven to 400 degrees with 10-inch cast-iron skillet in oven.
2. Whisk together flour, milk, sugar, cinnamon, salt, vanilla, and eggs in a medium bowl.
3. Remove skillet from oven and melt the butter in the pan, swirling pan to coat the base and sides with butter. Pour batter into the skillet and return to the oven.
4. Bake for 15 to 17 minutes.
5. Top with grapefruit, rosemary, and powdered sugar.

CHOCOLATE AND CRANBERRY BREAKFAST COOKIE

I am guilty of trying to sneak in desserts as breakfasts, but I have no reservations about these. I am completely earnest when I say they are a healthy way to eat a cookie for breakfast. And bonus, I never have to cajole my toddler into eating one on busy mornings.

Makes 12 cookies

1 1/2 cup quick-cooking oats

1/4 cup whole wheat flour

1/2 teaspoon salt

1/2 teaspoon baking soda

1 cup applesauce

1/4 cup maple syrup

1 teaspoon vanilla extract

1/3 cup chocolate chips

1/4 cup dried cranberries

1. Preheat oven to 350 degrees.
2. In a medium bowl stir together oats, flour, salt, and baking soda.
3. In a separate bowl mix applesauce, maple syrup, and vanilla.
4. Combine oat mixture and applesauce mixture. Fold in chocolate chips and cranberries.
5. Shape into 1 1/2-inch balls and arrange on a baking sheet at least 2 inches apart. Bake for 12 to 14 minutes.

Happy to Help: A Tip from My Friend

BATCH COOKING

In the past few years, my friend Carissa's family life has gone from plugging away at the predictable to braving some highly demanding circumstances. As she has dealt with three of her seven children's special needs relating to adoption and a major congenital heart defect, I have seen her personify steadfastness and perseverance. Keeping her family steady requires a lot of hard work, and I can confidently call her an expert on flexibility and managing expectations.

Carissa says, "With all the busyness that comes with our big family, one of my favorite things to do when I am cooking is to make extra to freeze for later." She has lots of tips for mastering the craft of batch cooking. When making spaghetti sauce or taco meat, double your recipe and make it last for two meals. For example, you can eat spaghetti now and freeze a spaghetti pie, or have tacos tonight and taco salad tomorrow. Extras from a large roast can become a beef stew, and a slow cooker full of chicken breasts shred and freeze nicely for future casseroles.

CARISSA'S GERMAN CREPES

Whipping up this breakfast is a tradition of Carissa's big German family, but it goes by its German name in their household—Blinna. It has even earned the status of favorite food by every one of her children! I like these crepes topped with jam and powdered sugar.

Serves 5 to 6

1 packet active dry yeast

1 cup warm water

3 cups all-purpose flour

1 teaspoon salt

2 tablespoons sugar

2 1/2 cups warm milk, divided

1/3 cup canola oil

3 large eggs, lightly beaten

Butter for greasing skillet

Optional toppings: sour cream, light brown sugar, jam, powdered sugar, butter

1. Dissolve yeast in 1 cup of warm water.
2. In a medium bowl whisk together yeast water, flour, salt, sugar, and 2 cups warm milk. Cover bowl with a towel and allow to rise 8 to 12 hours, or overnight, at room temperature.
3. The next day whisk 1/2 cup warm milk, oil, and eggs into the flour mixture. Allow to rise again for 30 minutes.
4. Pour 1/4 cup batter into a large greased skillet over medium heat. Lift pan from burner and swirl to spread batter thinly. Once bubbles form, flip and cook to a slight golden brown.
5. Add topping and roll crepe into a spiral.

BREAKFAST PITAS

Brinner is slang for having breakfast foods for dinner. This recipe reverses it and recreates your typical pita entrée as a complete morning meal. Perhaps we should call it Dreakfast? Whatever name you choose, you can skip the fork for this breakfast on the go.

Serves 2

1 avocado, mashed

2 pitas

1/2 cup arugula

4 large eggs, scrambled

1/2 cup shredded white Cheddar cheese

1/2 pound ground breakfast sausage, cooked

Hot sauce to taste

1. Spread mashed avocado onto pitas.
2. Layer with arugula, scrambled eggs, white Cheddar, and breakfast sausage. Top with hot sauce.

FLOURLESS YOGURT AND BANANA PANCAKES

Using bananas and yogurt as a base in these flourless pancakes makes them a healthy option without losing tastiness. This is especially popular with gluten-free friends.

Makes about 12 pancakes

2 very ripe bananas, plus banana for garnish

1/4 cup vanilla yogurt

4 large eggs

1/4 teaspoon ground cinnamon

1/4 teaspoon baking powder

1/2 teaspoon vanilla extract

Maple syrup

1. In a medium bowl mash the bananas.
2. Add yogurt, eggs, cinnamon, baking powder, and vanilla, then whisk together.
3. In a large skillet over medium heat, pour 1/4 cup batter into circles. Cook for 1 to 2 minutes on each side.
4. Serve with maple syrup and additional banana slices.

BREAKFAST CROISSANT SANDWICH

Finding a fast and nutritious breakfast is so difficult that sometimes I just give up and eat cake. (A whopping stack of pancakes basically has the same level of nutrients, right?) If you have a similar struggle but do not want to end up making a dessert for your breakfast, this easy-to-make, savory sandwich is a win.

Serves 3

1 tablespoon olive oil

3 cups fresh spinach

1 clove garlic, minced

A dash of ground nutmeg

1/4 teaspoon salt

1/4 teaspoon black pepper

3 croissants, sliced

3 large eggs, hard-boiled and sliced

1. Heat olive oil in a small skillet over medium-low heat. Add spinach and sauté with garlic, nutmeg, salt, and pepper until spinach is wilted.
2. Layer spinach on croissants and top with eggs.

BLUEBERRY CHEESECAKE STUFFED FRENCH TOAST

Many breakfast foods tend to be utilitarian, but sometimes it is nice to make something a bit fancy. When my husband eats this French toast, he says he feels like we are dining on a restaurant's breakfast specialty. This recipe can inspire that kind of awe with only a little effort.

Serves 3 to 4

1 cup blueberries

3 tablespoons sugar

1/2 cup water

1 (8-ounce) package cream cheese, softened

1/2 cup powdered sugar

3 large eggs

1/2 cup half-and-half

1 teaspoon vanilla extract

1/2 teaspoon ground cinnamon

1 loaf of sliced French bread

Butter for greasing skillet

Whipped topping

Maple syrup

1. In a small skillet over medium-high heat, combine blueberries with sugar and 1/2 cup water and bring to boil. Reduce heat to low and simmer for 10 minutes.
2. Puree blueberry sauce in a food processor with cream cheese and powdered sugar. Allow to cool for 10 minutes.
3. In a bowl whisk together eggs, half-and-half, vanilla, and cinnamon.
4. Slice bread into 1-inch thick slices, with a slit halfway through the center of each piece.
5. Using a spoon, stuff opening in bread with blueberry cheesecake filling.
6. Soak each side of a slice of bread in egg mixture. Grease skillet with butter. Toast bread for 1 to 2 minutes on each side in a large skillet over medium heat.
7. Top with whipped topping and maple syrup.

Happy to Help: A Tip from My Friend

HOSTING OVERNIGHT GUESTS

I have loved my friend Niki since we met on a trip overseas in college. She and her husband now live in that small European country where we met, and as expatriates, they often accommodate overnight guests. Never have I felt so comfortable traveling as I did when Niki hosted our family in her home.

Her best advice for giving guests this relief and ease is to consider what makes you comfortable when staying overnight. "My initial thoughts were having snacks easily accessible, cleanliness, and the attitude of the hosts," she says. When we arrived at her home, there was a welcome basket waiting for us with bottled water, local treats, and homemade chocolate chip cookies. A helpful note gave Internet information and phone numbers. It also informed us that our linens were freshly laundered, breakfast would be ready in the morning, and a shelf in the bathroom had been cleared for our toiletries.

Anticipating needs helps visitors feel like they truly can make themselves at home. Even living in her single-story, two-bedroom apartment (with a baby!), Niki has shown me what hospitality requires most is a warm heart and a desire to serve selflessly.

NIKI'S DARK CHOCOLATE SCONES

An almost unbelievable fact about Niki is that she received a children's chef coat when she was eight years old, and it still fits her today! She is a fantastic baker and has successfully converted me into a scone lover. These scones are best fresh out of the oven, so if you are going to be low on time, make the dough in advance. The dough can be frozen and then prepared as usual. No need to thaw; just add a few extra minutes to the baking time.

Makes 8 scones

2 cups all-purpose flour

1/4 cup firmly packed
light brown sugar

2 teaspoons baking powder

2 teaspoons ground cinnamon

1/2 teaspoon salt

6 tablespoons butter, cut
into half-inch cubes

2/3 cup milk, divided

1 cup dark chocolate chunks

Turbinado sugar

1. Preheat oven to 375 degrees.
2. In the bowl of an electric mixer combine flour, brown sugar, baking powder, cinnamon, and salt on low speed for 10 seconds. Add butter to bowl, continuing to mix until butter is evenly distributed in small crumbs.
3. Slowly pour milk into flour mixture and mix until incorporated, reserving about 1 tablespoon of milk. Fold chocolate chunks into dough.
4. Empty dough onto a flat surface and fold dough in half once vertically and horizontally to evenly incorporate chocolate. Roll dough into a 1-inch thick rectangle and transfer to parchment paper–lined baking sheet.
5. Spread the reserved 1 tablespoon of milk over top of dough and sprinkle with turbinado sugar.
6. Bake for 17 to 19 minutes. Allow to cool for 5 minutes before slicing into 8 triangles.

PUMPKIN AND PECAN BAKED OATMEAL

This filling breakfast is downright incredible. I love to make it the day after Thanksgiving. It is full of fall flavors and keeps us satisfied as we are lounging in our pajamas and putting up Christmas decorations.

Serves 5 to 6

2 cups quick-cooking oats

1 cup firmly packed light brown sugar

1 teaspoon baking powder

1 teaspoon ground cinnamon

1/2 teaspoon ground nutmeg

1/2 teaspoon salt

1/2 cup pumpkin puree

3/4 cup evaporated milk

1 teaspoon vanilla extract

1 large egg

1/2 cup chocolate chips

1/4 cup pecans

1. Preheat oven to 350 degrees.
2. In a large bowl stir together oats, brown sugar, baking powder, cinnamon, nutmeg, and salt.
3. In a separate bowl mix pumpkin puree, evaporated milk, vanilla, and egg.
4. Combine pumpkin puree mixture with oat mixture. Fold in chocolate chips.
5. Transfer batter to a greased 9 x 9-inch baking dish. Top with pecans. Bake for 35 minutes.

HERBED MINI QUICHES

Have you ever been eating a quiche and thought, I wish eating this were more convenient? Stop pondering that question because the answer is, "It can be!" These tiny, handheld quiches are another perfect on-the-go breakfast.

Makes 36 mini quiches

4 ounces butter crackers

2 tablespoons butter, melted

1 large egg white

3/4 cup grated Parmesan cheese, divided

2 (8-ounce) packages cream cheese, softened

1/4 teaspoon salt

1/4 teaspoon black pepper

1 teaspoon chopped fresh parsley, plus extra for garnish

1/4 teaspoon dried dill

3 large eggs

1/2 teaspoon lemon juice

1 teaspoon chopped chives

1. Preheat oven to 350 degrees.
2. In a food processor pulse together crackers, butter, egg white, and 1/4 cup Parmesan cheese. Press crumbs into bottom of cups of mini muffin pan. Bake crust for 6 to 8 minutes, until lightly brown.
3. In the food processor combine cream cheese, salt, pepper, 1/2 cup Parmesan, parsley, dill, eggs, and lemon juice.
4. Fold in chives and pour batter onto crusts.
5. Bake for 13 to 15 minutes. Top with additional parsley.

WHITE CHOCOLATE FRENCH TOAST KABOBS

Kabobs on the grill are my all-time favorite summer dinner. That devotion to kabobbing inspired me to create this breakfast rendition that children love helping to assemble. I cut up the fruit, and they get to skewer it. You can change things up by substituting or adding any seasonal fruit.

Serves 3 to 4

3/4 cup half-and-half

1 teaspoon vanilla extract

3 tablespoons butter, plus extra for skillet

2 tablespoons firmly packed light brown sugar

1/2 teaspoon ground cinnamon

1/4 teaspoon salt

2/3 cup white chocolate chips

3 large eggs

1 loaf of sliced French bread

Butter for greasing skillet

2 cups blackberries

3 peaches, sliced

Maple syrup

1. In a medium saucepan over low heat stir half-and-half, vanilla, butter, brown sugar, cinnamon, salt, and white chocolate until melted. Allow to cool.
2. In a bowl whisk eggs and incorporate into half-and-half mixture.
3. Soak each side of a slice of bread in egg mixture. Grease skillet with butter. Toast bread for 1 to 2 minutes on each side in a large skillet over medium heat. Repeat with remaining slices.
4. Slice French toast into 1-inch cubes. Assemble kabobs on skewers with French toast pieces, blackberries, and peaches. Drizzle with maple syrup.

MAPLE SWEET POTATO HASH BROWNS

This dish is a welcome change of pace from the usual oatmeal or cereal breakfast most of us eat every weekday. When glorious Saturday arrives, we unapologetically feast on this hearty, sweet, and savory meal.

Serves 3 to 4

8 cups water

3 sweet potatoes, cubed

1 pound bacon, cooked and chopped, with fat reserved

1/2 yellow onion, diced

1 teaspoon garlic powder

1/2 teaspoon red pepper flakes

Salt to taste

Black pepper to taste

4 large eggs, fried

Maple syrup

1. Bring a large pot of 8 cups water to boil over high heat. Add potatoes and reduce heat to medium. Cook for 10 minutes.
2. Heat reserved bacon fat in a large skillet over medium-high heat and then add the potatoes and the onion. Fry until the potatoes are crispy, about 10 to 12 minutes. Remove from heat and fold in cooked bacon. Season with garlic powder, red pepper flakes, salt, and pepper.
3. Top with fried eggs and drizzle with maple syrup.

SNACKS AND APPETIZERS

Sweet Potato and Roasted Grape Crostini

Carrot Bread

Apple Cookies

Toffee and Coconut Snack Bars

Avocado Deviled Eggs

Vanessa's Sweet Potato and Asparagus Salad

BBQ Chicken Pizza Bread

Loaded Skillet Fries

Watermelon and Pistachio Salad

Bean Quesadillas with Mango Salsa

Carolyn's Stuffed Mushrooms

Coconut Almond Chocolate Popcorn

Almond and Pear Baked Brie

Blueberry Cheese Ball

Raspberry Roasted Cheese Dip

TENDING TO MY GUESTS, BIG AND SMALL

We make a place for hospitality in our homes so we can build new relationships and love our friends well. I find one of the most important practical pieces of hospitality is caring for my littlest guests—the children. Because really, if the children's needs are accommodated, the parents' stress levels stay low, and they are free to engage in some grown-up time.

When having visitors, I avoid a table setting that makes anything seem too precious. Sometimes paper plates are better than bone china, and I say a jar of flowers always beats a crystal vase. If I am serving snacks, I might prepare both the Almond and Pear Baked Brie and the Coconut Almond Chocolate Popcorn so everybody is happy.

You can prepare your home for kid-guests beyond the dining table. To be honest, I think about this just about every time I buy something shiny and new for our house. Could it withstand an accidental bump from a chubby little elbow? Does it add to a welcoming atmosphere, or make me nervous about breakage? We prioritized making our outdoor eating area nice before working on other parts of our home. It is easier to host big groups there, and the outdoors dispels the we-must-keep-everything-clean vibe.

For the same reason, I keep a couple extra high chairs on hand. Many friends are willing to eat with young children in their laps, but it is a welcome relief to have baby gear available (and they will not need to drive over with a car full of equipment). If you do not have kids, you could keep it simple by having a few bibs and a stash of juice boxes in your cupboard. Offering a handful of toys and games to older children ensures they have something to interest them while parents are engaged in after-dinner conversation. (For warmer months, sidewalk chalk is one of the cheapest and most versatile options.) My motive in all of this is to make young people my guests just as much as their parents are.

Any parent will tell you they feel cared for when they see others taking an interest in their children. Kids are people too, of course, and their taste buds love attention. Even for my own kids, I aim to arrange our home and menus in a way that shows they are welcome additions in our family. I want to create a warm and inviting place for the honest, joyful, refreshing presence of children. Baking a loaf of carrot bread and carefully placing warm slices into tiny hands is a good gift for them and for me. They get to delight in a delicious treat, and I have the privilege of calling a host of little ones my friends.

SWEET POTATO AND ROASTED GRAPE CROSTINI

It was not too long ago that I realized how much I like sweet potatoes. As a person who pretty much always wants more sugar, I cannot believe I went without them for so long. They are probably the healthiest way to add an element of sweetness to any dish.

Makes about 20 crostinis

2 sweet potatoes

20 grapes, halved

1 tablespoon olive oil

$1/4$ teaspoon salt

$1/4$ teaspoon black pepper

1 tablespoon maple syrup

A dash of red pepper flakes

1 cup ricotta cheese

$1/2$ yellow onion, caramelized

1 loaf French bread, cut in $1/2$-inch thick slices and toasted

1. Preheat oven to 400 degrees.
2. Poke holes in sweet potatoes with a fork and bake for 45 minutes.
3. Place grapes in a bowl, drizzle with olive oil, and season with salt and black pepper. Arrange on a parchment paper-lined baking sheet. Add to oven with sweet potatoes and roast for 20 minutes.
4. Remove inside of roasted sweet potatoes from skin and mash in a bowl. Stir in maple syrup and red pepper flakes.
5. Assemble crostini by layering ricotta, sweet potato, caramelized onions, and roasted grapes over toasted bread.

CARROT BREAD

Depending on what kind of person you are, you could have this quick bread by itself and probably enjoy some semblance of health and wellness, or you could slather it with cream cheese frosting. (Full disclosure, I am the frosting type!)

Makes 2 loaves

5 carrots, peeled, steamed, pureed, and cooled

2 large eggs

1/2 cup canola oil

1/4 cup milk

1 teaspoon vanilla extract

1 3/4 cups all-purpose flour

1 cup sugar

1/2 cup firmly packed light brown sugar

2 teaspoons baking soda

1 teaspoon ground cinnamon

1/2 teaspoon ground nutmeg

1/4 teaspoon salt

Cream Cheese Frosting (recipe on page 226)

1. Preheat oven to 350 degrees.
2. Combine mashed carrots with eggs, canola oil, milk, and vanilla in the bowl of an electric mixer on medium-low speed for about 1 minute. Take caution that the mashed carrot is not so warm that it cooks the eggs.
3. In a separate bowl stir together flour, sugar, brown sugar, baking soda, cinnamon, nutmeg, and salt.
4. Slowly incorporate the flour mixture into the carrot mixture, continuing to mix until combined.
5. Transfer batter to 2 greased 9 x 5-inch loaf pans. Bake for 45 minutes.
6. Cover with foil and bake for a final 15 minutes.
7. Cool and frost with cream cheese frosting.

APPLE COOKIES

During my first pregnancy, I craved apples in a manner I believe is unequal
to anyone who has ever walked the earth. My sweet husband often made
these for me to satisfy my cravings. With the addition of nuts for protein,
this snack is perfectly filling—a good way to fight off feeling hangry.

Makes 8 cookies

1 Honeycrisp apple

¼ cup peanut butter

¼ cup almonds, sliced

¼ cup walnuts, chopped

¼ cup sweetened shredded coconut

¼ cup chocolate chips

1. Slice apple into 8 thin rings and remove core. Spread peanut butter over one side of each ring.
2. Top with the almonds, walnuts, coconut, and chocolate chips.

TOFFEE AND COCONUT SNACK BARS

With the fresh-from-the-oven warm, gooey sweetness of these little delights, you will want them for breakfast, an afternoon snack, and even dessert. World, please meet my granola bar soul mate.

Makes 9 bars

1 3/4 cups quick-cooking oats

1 cup crisp rice cereal

1/4 cup sweetened shredded coconut

1/2 cup chocolate chunks

1/2 cup toffee pieces

1/3 cup firmly packed light brown sugar

1/4 cup (1/2 stick) butter, softened

1/2 cup peanut butter

1/4 cup honey

1 teaspoon vanilla extract

1 large egg

1. Preheat oven to 350 degrees.
2. Combine oats, cereal, coconut, chocolate, toffee, brown sugar, butter, peanut butter, honey, vanilla, and egg in a large bowl. Press mixture into a greased 9 x 9-inch baking dish.
3. Bake 18 to 20 minutes, until golden brown. Allow to cool and slice into bars.

AVOCADO DEVILED EGGS

I am in the extremely small club of Midwesterners who are afraid of mayonnaise. It took me awhile to figure out how to create some classic dishes without it, but I got there. I am proud to present mayo-less deviled eggs. Even the most ardent mayo-lovers would not want to resist these.

Makes 12 deviled eggs

6 large eggs, hard-boiled, peeled, and halved

1/2 avocado

1 teaspoon lime juice

Pinch of red pepper flakes

1 teaspoon red wine vinegar

1 tablespoon olive oil

1/4 teaspoon garlic salt

Black pepper to taste

1/4 cup bacon, crumbled

1. Remove yolks from eggs and mash yolks in a bowl with avocado, lime juice, red pepper flakes, red wine vinegar, olive oil, and garlic salt.
2. Use a piping bag (or plastic bag with a small hole cut on the corner) to place the filling in the egg whites. Top with black pepper and bacon crumbles.

Happy to Help: A Tip from My Friend

INCLUDING CHILDREN IN HOSPITALITY

One of the most remarkable things about my friend Vanessa is that even with young children, her house is characterized by a feeling of peace. Until another friend pointed it out to me, I had not realized that I have never seen her house in chaos, even though I have dropped by many times!

I think what has allowed her to create such a peaceful home is how she brings her children into her tasks with her. She says her goal is not just for her and her husband to be hospitable but rather for her whole family to be.

Her kids love decorating little cards with the name of each guest and placing them around the table. While she is preparing food (and maybe letting the kids help with cooking jobs too), she talks with them about the guests coming over. Together they think of questions to ask: What was your favorite food growing up? How many siblings do you have? What is your favorite thing about autumn? She says, "These all may seem like basic questions, but this kind of intentional communication helps train little ones in the art of conversation."

Her family beautifully shows they care about people and the specifics of their lives, and her young ones are learning to love hospitality.

VANESSA'S SWEET POTATO AND ASPARAGUS SALAD

Vanessa once told me she realized her three-year-old knew the word homemade *when he insisted on having only his mom's homemade dressing with his vegetables! That delicious dressing recipe is right at home in this inventive salad.*

Serves 3 to 4

1 sweet potato, peeled and diced

3 tablespoons water

5 asparagus stems, sliced into thirds

2 tablespoons plus 1 cup
olive oil, divided

1/2 teaspoon salt, divided

1/2 teaspoon black pepper, divided

1/2 cup balsamic vinegar

2 garlic cloves

2 tablespoons stone-ground mustard

2 teaspoons sugar

6 cups field greens

1 cup red cabbage, sliced thinly

1/2 cup thinly sliced red onion

1/3 cup walnuts

1/2 cup crumbled blue cheese

1. Preheat oven to broil.
2. Place sweet potatoes in a bowl with 3 tablespoons water and microwave for 3 1/2 minutes on high.
3. Toss sweet potatoes and asparagus in a plastic bag with 2 tablespoons olive oil, 1/4 teaspoon salt, and 1/4 teaspoon pepper.
4. Spread vegetables onto a parchment paper–lined baking sheet. Broil for 10 minutes.
5. Prepare dressing by whisking 1 cup olive oil, balsamic vinegar, garlic, mustard, sugar, 1/4 teaspoon salt, and 1/4 teaspoon pepper together in a bowl.
6. Assemble salad by tossing together the field greens, cabbage, roasted vegetables, red onion, walnuts, blue cheese, and dressing.

BBQ CHICKEN PIZZA BREAD

My husband's very favorite pizza is BBQ chicken. That means one of my jobs as Dinner Maker in Chief is to find different ways for him to enjoy said pizza. This snack bread has become a must for sports-watching parties.

Serves 3 to 4

1 pound pizza dough

½ cup barbecue sauce

¼ red onion, diced

2 chicken breasts, cooked and shredded

2 cups shredded mozzarella cheese, divided

2 tablespoons fresh cilantro, chopped

1. Preheat oven to 350 degrees.
2. Roll out pizza dough into a rectangle. Layer with barbecue sauce, red onion, chicken, and 1 cup mozzarella.
3. Cut rectangle into 6 strips and stack strips onto each other (sauce side facing up). Slice stack of strips into 6 square stacks.
4. Place stacks on their side in a greased 5 x 9-inch loaf pan. Sprinkle with remaining 1 cup mozzarella. Bake for 30 to 35 minutes. Top with cilantro.

LOADED SKILLET FRIES

If you are up for the high-commitment, long-term relationship of maintaining a cast-iron skillet, you simply must try serving fries this way. (For my cast-iron skillet care, I only clean it with coarse salt, water, and a bristled brush.) Boring meat and potatoes, be gone!

Serves 3 to 4

2 pounds Russet potatoes, sliced

4 tablespoons olive oil, divided

1 teaspoon salt, divided

1 teaspoon black pepper, divided

1/4 teaspoon garlic powder

1/4 teaspoon dried oregano

1 red bell pepper, sliced

1 yellow bell pepper, sliced

1 orange bell pepper, sliced

1 yellow onion, sliced

1 pound flank steak

1/2 cup grated Parmesan cheese

2 tablespoons Blue Cheese Sauce (recipe on page 144)

1 tablespoon chives, chopped

1. Preheat oven to 450 degrees.
2. Arrange sliced potatoes on a parchment paper–lined baking sheet. Drizzle with 2 tablespoons olive oil and season with 1/2 teaspoon salt, 1/2 teaspoon black pepper, garlic powder, and oregano.
3. On a second baking sheet, drizzle bell peppers and onions with 1 tablespoon olive oil.
4. Roast both pans in the oven for 40 to 45 minutes, flipping the fries halfway through.
5. Drizzle the flank steak with 1 tablespoon olive oil and season with remaining 1/2 teaspoon salt and remaining 1/2 teaspoon black pepper.
6. In a large skillet over medium heat, sear each side of the steak for 2 to 3 minutes. Transfer to a cutting board. Cover with foil and let rest for 10 minutes. Slice into strips.
7. Transfer baked fries into a 10-inch cast-iron skillet. Top with Parmesan. Broil in oven until cheese melts, about 2 to 3 minutes.
8. Top with steak, peppers, onions, blue cheese dressing, and chives.

WATERMELON AND PISTACHIO SALAD

*One of my favorite summer snacks is watermelon sprinkled with
a little salt. The salt magnifies the melon's sweetness, so a salad
like this brings even more depth to the flavor relationship.*

Serves 3 to 4

1 tablespoon honey

1 cup balsamic vinegar

6 cups cubed or balled watermelon

1/2 teaspoon mint, chopped

1 avocado, diced

1/2 cup pistachios

2 teaspoons olive oil

1/2 cup crumbled feta cheese

Salt to taste

Black pepper to taste

1. Bring honey and balsamic vinegar
   to boil in a small skillet over high
   heat. Reduce to medium-low heat
   and simmer for 10 to 15 minutes, until
   mixture is reduced by about half.
   Remove from heat and allow to cool.

2. Place watermelon, mint, avocado, and
   pistachios in a bowl and toss together.
   Drizzle with olive oil and balsamic
   reduction.

3. Top with feta. Season with salt and
   pepper.

BEAN QUESADILLAS WITH MANGO SALSA

These quesadillas are a snack for my husband and me when our babies are asleep and we are staying up late watching a movie. They are also a healthy treat or lunch option for kids and a perfect dish to serve when vegetarian friends drop by.

Makes 8 quesadillas

Butter for greasing skillet

8 (8-inch) flour tortillas

2 cups shredded pepper jack cheese

1 yellow onion, sliced and caramelized

2 cups black beans

1 mango, diced

1 tablespoon lime juice

Pinch of salt

2 tablespoons fresh cilantro

1 teaspoon jalapeño, minced

1/4 teaspoon red pepper flakes (optional)

1/4 teaspoon sugar

1 teaspoon sriracha sauce

1. Lightly grease a large skillet with butter and heat to medium-low.
2. Lay a tortilla onto pan and spread a layer of pepper jack cheese. Top with onion and black beans on half of the tortilla. Toast the tortilla for about 2 minutes. Fold in half. Remove from heat and slice into thirds.
3. Repeat steps 1 and 2 to make seven more quesadillas.
4. Prepare salsa by mixing together the mango, lime juice, salt, cilantro, jalapeño, red pepper flakes, and sugar in a bowl.
5. Serve quesadillas with mango salsa and sriracha sauce.

Happy to Help: A Tip from My Friend

CREATING DEPTH OF FLAVOR IN VEGETARIAN DISHES

As firm meat-avores, David and I were mystified and intrigued when our friend Carolyn told us that she eats meatless dinners most nights. Everything she has ever cooked for us had been delightful (even sans meat!), and I was enticed by the budget-saving potential. Carolyn shared with me her secrets on how to go meatless without going flavorless.

It starts with knowing that making a successful vegetarian meal does not mean merely omitting the meat from a recipe. Carolyn says, "The key to an excellent vegetarian meal worthy of second helpings is building depth of flavor." She has some smart ideas to do this—tossing toasted almonds or walnuts into a pasta dish, sautéing vegetables with aromatics like ginger or crushed garlic, deglazing a pan with vegetable stock, or stirring reconstituted dried mushrooms into a warm soup.

By keeping a few strategic ingredients on hand, we can prepare flavorful and completely meatless entrées as often as we please.

CAROLYN'S STUFFED MUSHROOMS

Carolyn first made this mushroom recipe one Thanksgiving when she wanted to prepare a special appetizer for her newly vegetarian brother. Now it has become a family tradition to make a huge batch every year. When you try it, you will know why.

Makes about 60 mushrooms

3 shallots, minced

2 tablespoons butter

45 ounces white mushrooms

A dash of salt

4 cloves garlic, minced

1 tablespoon tomato paste

2 teaspoons soy sauce

1 cup walnuts, chopped and toasted

1 (8-ounce) package cream cheese

1 cup bread crumbs

1/3 cup grated Parmesan cheese

1 teaspoon fresh rosemary, chopped

1 teaspoon fresh thyme

1 teaspoon olive oil

1. Preheat oven to 350 degrees.
2. Sauté shallots with butter in a large skillet over medium heat for 3 to 5 minutes, until tender.
3. Remove the stems from the mushroom caps. Pulse stems in a food processor until finely chopped. Season with a dash of salt. Add to skillet and cook until softened, about 6 minutes.
4. Add the garlic, tomato paste, and soy sauce and cook for 1 minute.
5. Remove pan from heat and incorporate the walnuts and cream cheese.
6. In a bowl combine the bread crumbs, Parmesan, rosemary, thyme, and olive oil. Spoon filling into mushroom caps. Top with bread crumb mixture.
7. Arrange the stuffed mushrooms on a parchment paper-lined baking sheet and bake for 25 to 30 minutes.

COCONUT ALMOND CHOCOLATE POPCORN

It is always fun to involve kids in preparing popcorn. They love helping measure and pour and watching the first kernels sizzle and spring open. And when we spruce up the popcorn with special sweets, they are even more jazzed. Throwing in a bit of salt here makes the sweetness really pop (pun intended). If you are short on time, you can make microwave popcorn and skip to step 3 below.

Makes about 6 cups

1/2 cup coconut oil, divided

3/4 cup uncooked popcorn

2 cups chocolate chips

1 1/2 cups sweetened shredded coconut

1 1/2 cups sliced almonds

1/2 teaspoon salt

1. Melt 1/4 cup coconut oil in a large pot that has a lid over medium heat. Once oil is melted, add 3 popcorn kernels and cover. Once kernels have popped, remove from heat and add the rest of the kernels.

2. Cover again with the lid cracked and return to medium-high heat for about 2 minutes, shaking pot frequently.

3. Meanwhile, melt chocolate with 1/4 cup coconut oil in microwave on half power, stirring every 30 seconds until smooth.

4. Toss cooked popcorn in the chocolate and spread out on a parchment paper–lined flat surface to dry. Once chocolate has hardened, sprinkle in coconut, sliced almonds, and salt.

ALMOND AND PEAR BAKED BRIE

I hope this will not alienate Brie lovers, but I cannot enjoy the beloved dessert cheese unless it is warm and melty. This combination of warm Brie and sweet, tart pears might make you feel warm and melty inside too.

Serves 3 to 4

2 pears, cubed

2 tablespoons firmly packed light brown sugar

2 tablespoons butter

8 ounces Brie

1 tablespoon sliced almonds

1/4 teaspoon ground cinnamon

Baguette

1. Preheat oven to 350 degrees.
2. In a medium skillet over medium heat, sauté pears with brown sugar and butter for 11 to 13 minutes, until the pears are tender.
3. Place the Brie on a parchment paper-lined baking sheet. Bake for 13 to 15 minutes.
4. Top the Brie with the sautéed pears, almonds, and cinnamon. Serve with sliced baguette.

BLUEBERRY CHEESE BALL

If you are a person who wonders if the macaroni crafts you did as a child prepared you for life, then this cheese ball is for you. With that experience you (and your children) are already highly skilled and ready to gingerly place blueberries on this delicious ball of goat cheese. I have yet to taste anything involving goat cheese that I did not like.

Serves 5 to 6

8 ounces goat cheese

4 cloves garlic, roasted

1/4 teaspoon black pepper

1/4 teaspoon onion powder

1/2 teaspoon honey

6 ounces blueberries

Toasted bread

1. In a bowl mash together the goat cheese, roasted garlic, pepper, onion powder, and honey.
2. Shape ingredients into a ball. Press the blueberries into the cheese. Serve with toasted bread.

RASPBERRY ROASTED CHEESE DIP

Strictly speaking, this is an appetizer, but I must admit we have eaten bite after bite (after bite) until it became our whole lunch. Fruit and cheese are total best friends for life, so they just had to be put into a roasted dip together.

Serves 5 to 6

½ teaspoon Dijon mustard

1 (8-ounce) package cream cheese, softened

1 teaspoon black pepper

2 teaspoon balsamic vinegar

½ cup plain Greek yogurt

¼ teaspoon ground cinnamon

1 tablespoon honey

1 cup grated Parmesan cheese

1 cup shredded Monterey Jack cheese

2 cups raspberries

Toasted bread

1. Preheat oven to 350 degrees.
2. In a large bowl mix together the Dijon, cream cheese, pepper, balsamic vinegar, Greek yogurt, cinnamon, and honey. Fold in the Parmesan, Monterey Jack, and raspberries.
3. Spread mixture into a 9 x 9-inch greased baking dish. Bake for 35 to 40 minutes. Serve with toasted bread.

ENTRÉES

Prosciutto Sandwich with Apricot Spread

Spaghetti Squash Burrito Bowls

Hawaiian Slow Cooker Chicken

Fajita Grilled Cheese

Southwestern Stuffed Peppers

Avocado Pesto Pasta

Apple Cider Beef Stew

Jenny's Mushroom Braciole

Chicken Fried Rice

Chicken Tortilla Soup

Chicken Lo Mein

Feta and Spinach Stuffed Shells

Balsamic Pesto Chicken with Quinoa

Apple Mac and Gouda

Spaghetti Squash Pad Thai

Chicken Noodle Soup

Barley Vegetable Bowl

Shepherd's Pie Cakes

Brad's Spatchcock Chicken

BLT Pizza

Beet and Kale Lasagna Roll-Ups

Ham and Swiss Hand Pies

Plum Caprese Stuffed Pork Loin

Butternut Squash Goulash

Loaded Baked Potato Gnocchi

I KNOW WHAT'S FOR DINNER!

There was a time in our marriage when David and I went out to eat sushi almost every Saturday. You guessed it: we did not yet have kids. Those excursions gave us special memories, but my goodness—the cost! I am no small advocate for meal planning, and hitting our stride in this area has cut down on the urge to eat out every few days and given a boost to the budget.

The benefits of meal planning are compelling. Taking a tiny bit of time to think ahead pays off in dividends—and it is easy. First, it saves you three billion dollars a month. Not really, but seriously, the savings are significant. We are convinced that when we wander into a store grabbing whatever looks good with no specific meals in mind, we walk out with a load of expensive snack food (and probably a trampoline and three goldfish).

Second, no one likes the stress of already feeling hungry and having to utter, "What should we have for dinner tonight?" To keep this from happening, I started spending one hour on Fridays choosing the meals for the entire week, making a grocery list, and figuring out which ingredients I can use for multiple meals. Everyone is tended to, nourished, and (usually) happy. If you struggle to look forward to cooking, this will certainly help boost morale.

Having a menu planned solves other problems too. We eat healthier because we snack less when we know what we will eat and when. We get truly full at our premeditated, complete meals instead of having to scavenge for croutons and shredded coconut to eat a makeshift dinner. Also, the family always knows what is for dinner, which is nice for them (and one less question I have to field).

As much as I love plans, I know they are not infallible. A weeknight event emerges abruptly, or I forgot to buy a key ingredient and end up going to the store for just one thing (the worst!). Or I burn the casserole beyond possible consumption and have to pull something else together. Such is life. These inconveniences keep us from having too tight a grip on these little efforts of ours. Even with the possibility of plans unraveling, we keep looking for ways to establish our household and support it well for the ones we love.

If you have never made a meal plan in your life, do not feel bad—or assume I am saying this makes you some sort of sluggard! My point is: you may find that if you are like me, there are some things that will just never happen (or not happen well) if you do not plan for them. You might love how much easier cooking dinner becomes with just a little front-end work.

PROSCIUTTO SANDWICH
WITH APRICOT SPREAD

This surprisingly easy-to-make sandwich could liven up a boring weekday lunch routine, or you could serve them open-faced as little appetizers. It took me longer to learn how to pronounce prosciutto than it did to make these.

Makes 4 sandwiches

½ cup dried apricots

3 tablespoons olive oil

½ teaspoon balsamic vinegar

Pinch of salt

8 slices wheat bread

8 slices prosciutto

8 stalks roasted asparagus
(optional, recipe on page 154)

4 slices Havarti cheese

1. Puree the dried apricots, olive oil, balsamic vinegar, and salt in a food processor.
2. Assemble the sandwiches by spreading the apricot mixture on one side of four pieces of bread.
3. Layer with the prosciutto, roasted asparagus, and Havarti. Top with second piece of bread.

SPAGHETTI SQUASH BURRITO BOWLS

*At the beginning of our marriage, I made a spaghetti squash entrée that was
a bit of a flop and scared us away from the squash for some time. Eventually I
became brave enough to try it again when I had the idea to use them as burrito
bowls. We got back in the saddle—and our weeknight dinners are better for it.*

Serves 4

2 spaghetti squash, halved vertically

1 yellow onion, sliced

1 red bell pepper, sliced

1 orange bell pepper, sliced

1 tablespoon olive oil

1 lime, juiced

1 pound ground turkey

1 (15-ounce) can black beans, drained

1 (15-ounce) can corn, drained

2 tablespoons Mexican Seasoning
(recipe on page 158)

1 cup shredded Mexican cheese blend

1/4 cup fresh cilantro

1. Preheat oven to 400 degrees.
2. Lay spaghetti squash in a glass 9 x 13-inch baking dish. Roast for 40 minutes.
3. Place the onion and peppers in a second 9 x 13-inch baking dish and drizzle with olive oil. Add to oven with the squash and roast for 15 minutes. Top peppers and onions with lime juice.
4. Brown the turkey with Mexican seasoning in a large skillet over medium heat until cooked throughout. Stir in black beans and corn.
5. Using a spoon, remove the squash from its peel. Stir squash together with turkey, black beans, corn, peppers, and onion.
6. Fill squash shells with mixture. Top with the cheese and cilantro.

HAWAIIAN SLOW COOKER CHICKEN

My primary recipe taster is my husband because he is more adventurous than my toddler (and more articulate). His favorite part of this dish is what he has dubbed the "flavor bombs," also known as pineapple.

Serves 3 to 4

4 chicken breasts

2 tablespoons coconut oil

1 cup cubed pineapple

1 white onion, sliced

1 poblano pepper, sliced

½ cup barbecue sauce

½ cup teriyaki sauce

2 cups cooked brown rice

¼ cup fresh cilantro

1. Place the chicken, coconut oil, pineapple, onion, poblano pepper, barbecue sauce, and teriyaki sauce in slow cooker. Cook on low for 5 to 6 hours.
2. Serve over brown rice and top with cilantro.

FAJITA GRILLED CHEESE

The smell of onions simmering in a pan is one of my favorite smells in the world. I include them in every meal I can, and I sometimes even add extra in this dish. While traditional fajitas are not an on-the-go meal, the grilled cheese makes this version tidy and portable.

Serves 3 to 4

1 white onion, sliced

1 green bell pepper, sliced

1 red bell pepper, sliced

3 chicken breasts, sliced

2 tablespoons olive oil

2 tablespoons Mexican Seasoning (recipe on page 158)

1 lime, juiced

1 loaf Italian bread, sliced

2 cups shredded Cheddar cheese

Butter for greasing skillet

Guacamole

1. Preheat oven to 400 degrees.
2. Place onion, peppers, and chicken in 9 x 13-inch baking dish. Drizzle with olive oil. Sprinkle with Mexican seasoning and toss to coat.
3. Roast in oven 25 minutes. Remove from oven and top with lime juice.
4. Assemble the grilled cheese by layering the bread, cheese, chicken, vegetables, another layer of cheese, and top slice of bread.
5. Grill in a large, buttered skillet over medium heat for 2 to 3 minutes on each side (or grill in a panini press). Serve with guacamole.

SOUTHWESTERN STUFFED PEPPERS

This vegetable-oriented recipe is a nice, healthy version of Mexican cuisine. Slicing the peppers in half vertically makes them simpler to stuff, prettier on the plate, and easier to get into your mouth (which is always my main goal).

Serves 3 to 4

4 bell peppers, cores and seeds removed, sliced in half vertically

1 cup brown rice

1 1/2 cups water

1 cup salsa

1 pound ground turkey, cooked

1 (15-ounce) can black beans, drained

1 (15-ounce) can corn, drained

1 clove garlic, minced

3 tablespoons Mexican Seasoning (recipe on page 158)

1 cup shredded Cheddar cheese

1/4 cup chopped fresh cilantro

3 green onions, sliced

1. Preheat oven to 425 degrees.
2. Arrange peppers in a 9 x 13-inch baking dish and roast for 15 minutes.
3. In a medium saucepan over high heat bring the brown rice to boil with 1 1/2 cups water. Reduce heat to low. Cover pot and simmer for 10 to 12 minutes.
4. In a large bowl combine the salsa, cooked ground turkey, rice, black beans, corn, garlic, and Mexican seasoning.
5. Stuff roasted peppers with filling. Cover with aluminum foil and roast for 15 minutes.
6. Remove foil and sprinkle tops with the Cheddar. Roast for 5 more minutes.
7. Top with cilantro and green onion.

AVOCADO PESTO PASTA

Putting pesto on pasta is not new, but it is always a winner. I love bringing more variety to our pasta dishes in rotation, and this recipe delivers big flavor using only a few ingredients. Blending in an avocado to make your sauce silky smooth is a little trick that health-ifies things too.

Serves 3 to 4

2 cups Walnut Pesto (recipe on page 142)

1 avocado

1 pound Gemelli pasta, cooked al dente

3 chicken breasts, cooked and shredded

¼ cup grated Parmesan cheese

1. In a food processor add the pesto and avocado and pulse until creamy.
2. Toss avocado pesto with the cooked pasta and chicken in a large serving bowl. Top with Parmesan.

APPLE CIDER BEEF STEW

Having something prepped in advance on Sundays is a must for me so I do not get too crazy-hungry after church. Soups are one of my favorite ways to do it. Make this ahead and freeze it to enjoy later—maybe on a pleasant afternoon while watching football. Crisp apple cider is one of my favorites in autumn, and it brings a lovely, subtle sweetness to this stew.

Serves 5 to 6

10 Yukon Gold potatoes, diced

2 tablespoons olive oil

1 teaspoon salt

1 teaspoon black pepper

1 pound stew beef

1 sweet Vidalia onion, sliced

4 carrots, sliced

2 cloves garlic, minced

1/4 teaspoon chopped fresh parsley

1/2 teaspoon onion powder

1/2 teaspoon garlic salt

6 cups vegetable broth

1 cup apple cider

1 cup green peas

1 cup quick barley

Wheat baguette

1. Place the potatoes in a large pot, toss with olive oil, and season with salt and pepper. Cook over medium heat for 10 minutes, stirring frequently.
2. Add the stew beef and cook for 5 more minutes.
3. Stir in onion and carrots, cooking for an additional 5 minutes.
4. Add the garlic, parsley, onion powder, garlic salt, vegetable broth, and apple cider to pot. Reduce heat to low and simmer for 40 to 50 minutes.
5. Stir in the peas and barley. Cook for 2 to 3 more minutes. Serve with wheat baguette.

Happy to Help: A Tip from My Friend

TENDERIZING MEAT

I will not soon forget the warmth, order, and comfort I felt the first time we had dinner at my friend Jenny's house. There is something about her home that feels safe both for visitors and the ones living there. On the drive home I remember telling David their home seemed like the perfect place to get to be a kid: comfortable, lived-in, well-ordered, and lots of loving little details throughout. And to top it off, the food was downright fantastic.

Her biggest tip to bring this warm feeling to festive occasions is to pay attention to the details. Along with a linen napkin and nice place setting, she is savvy in the art and science of tenderizing meat—a detail that is easy to overlook, but worth remembering.

"There are a few ways to do this: heat, acid, salt, or pounding. All of these share the same goal of breaking down the fibers of the cut to make for a more tender bite," Jenny says. Many would reach for a meat mallet, but she showed me that your standard iron skillet works even better. Layer a steak between two slices of parchment paper and pound it with the skillet to tenderize both sides. This will create an even thickness so the meat cooks perfectly and consistently throughout.

JENNY'S MUSHROOM BRACIOLE

For a dish that really impresses, Jenny's braciole is the one to go for. It pairs nicely with red-skin potatoes or green beans and (somehow!) tastes even better than it looks.

Serves 3 to 4

2 cloves garlic, minced

8 baby bella mushrooms, sliced thinly

3 tablespoons chopped fresh parsley, plus extra for garnish

¹/₄ cup grated Parmesan, plus extra for garnish

1 large egg, lightly beaten

¹/₂ teaspoon salt

¹/₂ teaspoon black pepper

2 pounds flank steak, butterflied (cut in half parallel to cutting board almost all the way through, then lay out like a butterfly)

5 slices prosciutto

Kitchen twine

2 tablespoons olive oil, divided

1. Preheat oven to 350 degrees.
2. In a bowl stir together the garlic, mushrooms, parsley, Parmesan, egg, salt, and pepper.
3. Tenderize the steak and season both sides with salt and pepper. Line meat with prosciutto, covering all but the last 2 inches of one long side.
4. Arrange the mushroom filling on the other long side. Starting with that end, tightly roll meat. Tie steak closed with kitchen twine. Drizzle 1 tablespoon olive oil over roll.
5. Heat 1 tablespoon olive oil in a large cast-iron skillet over high heat. Brown the roll on all sides.
6. Transfer skillet to oven and roast for 25 to 30 minutes.
7. Place steak on cutting board and cover loosely with foil. Let rest for 10 minutes.
8. Slice the meat into 8 sections. Drizzle with the olive oil and top with Parmesan and parsley.

CHICKEN FRIED RICE

I really like having fresh Chinese food for dinner, but I rarely want to put up the cash to have take-out delivered. This is my version of the famous dish, not that I have any claim on what is authentic Chinese food. I am an authority, however, on what is super yummy.

Serves 3 to 4

1 cup brown rice

1 1/2 cups water

3 tablespoons sesame oil

1 white onion, chopped

2 cloves garlic, minced

1/2 cup frozen peas

1/2 cup carrots, diced

2 large eggs

3 chicken breasts, cooked and shredded

1/4 cup soy sauce

1. Bring brown rice to boil with the water in a medium saucepan over high heat. Reduce heat to low. Cover the pot and simmer for 10 to 12 minutes.

2. Heat sesame oil in a large skillet over medium heat. Add the onion, garlic, peas, and carrots. Cook for 5 to 7 minutes, until vegetables are tender.

3. Crack eggs into pan and scramble, mixing with vegetables. Add the rice, chicken, and soy sauce to pan. Stir to combine and remove from heat.

CHICKEN TORTILLA SOUP

This hearty chicken tortilla soup has lots of flavor and not too much broth. It is a dinner I often make in double batches. I will freeze a portion so we can have an easy meal later, or I might take half to a new mom who could use a break.

Serves 3 to 4

1 yellow onion, diced

2 cloves garlic, minced

2 tablespoons coconut oil

1 chipotle pepper (canned in adobo sauce), diced

1 red bell pepper, diced

2 tablespoons Mexican Seasoning (recipe on page 158)

1 (15-ounce) can corn, drained

1 (15-ounce) can black beans, drained

1 tablespoon adobo sauce (from canned chipotle pepper)

3 chicken breasts, cooked and shredded

1 lime, juiced

6 cups vegetable broth

1/4 cup fresh cilantro

Tortilla chips

Limes

1. Sauté onions with garlic and coconut oil in a large pot over medium heat for 5 minutes.
2. Add the chipotle pepper, bell pepper, and Mexican seasoning, cooking for 3 more minutes.
3. Add the corn, black beans, adobo sauce, shredded chicken, lime juice, and vegetable broth to pot. Reduce heat to low. Simmer for 20 minutes.
4. Serve with cilantro, tortilla chips, and lime wedges.

CHICKEN LO MEIN

One-pot meals are music to my ears on busy days when I have been running lots of errands. They also call my name on lazy days at home. Basically, I am down for a one-pot wonder anytime. You can make this one even easier by using precooked (or leftover) chicken.

Serves 3 to 4

2 cups water

2 cups vegetable broth

3 chicken breasts, cubed

12 ounces fettucine pasta

2 cloves garlic, minced

1 red bell pepper, sliced

4 carrots, sliced

2 teaspoons sugar

1/2 teaspoon sriracha sauce

3 tablespoons soy sauce

1 tablespoon sesame oil

2 teaspoons rice wine vinegar

1/4 teaspoon red pepper flakes

1/2 teaspoon onion powder

3/4 cup peas

3 green onions, sliced

1. Bring the water and vegetable broth to a boil in a large pot over high heat. Reduce to low heat and add chicken, simmering for 10 minutes.
2. Add the fettuccine, garlic, bell pepper, carrots, sugar, sriracha sauce, soy sauce, sesame oil, rice wine vinegar, red pepper flakes, and onion powder to pot. Increase heat to medium-high and bring to boil, stirring occasionally for 8 to 9 minutes.
3. Add peas and cook for 1 minute. Strain any excess liquid and top with green onion.

FETA AND SPINACH STUFFED SHELLS

I once (perhaps irrationally) was intimidated by making stuffed shells; something about them seemed intricate and difficult. I am not intimidated anymore, and you do not have to be either! I recommend this dish to anyone who likes easy and tasty Italian food.

Serves 3 to 4

2 tablespoons olive oil

1/2 yellow onion, diced

1 1/2 cups spinach

2 cloves garlic, minced

1 1/2 cups ricotta cheese

1 large egg

1 1/2 cups shredded mozzarella cheese

2 ounces crumbled feta cheese

1/2 cup walnuts, chopped

1/2 lemon, zested

2 teaspoons Italian Seasoning (recipe on page 160)

6 ounces jumbo shells, cooked al dente

3 cups tomato sauce

1/2 cup grated Parmesan cheese

2 tablespoons chives, chopped

1. Preheat oven to 350 degrees.
2. Heat the olive oil in a large skillet over medium heat and sauté onion for 4 to 5 minutes, until onion is tender. Add spinach and garlic, cooking until spinach is slightly wilted.
3. In a bowl combine spinach mixture with the ricotta, egg, mozzarella, feta, walnuts, lemon zest, and Italian seasoning.
4. Spoon filling into cooked shells and arrange in a 9 x 13-inch baking dish. Pour tomato sauce over shells.
5. Cover with aluminum foil and bake for 20 minutes.
6. Remove foil and bake 10 more minutes. Top with Parmesan and chives.

BALSAMIC PESTO CHICKEN WITH QUINOA

Balsamic vinegar + pesto + nutty quinoa = one of our very favorite dinners. I delight in being able to pop lots of elements of a dinner into the oven, all in the same pan.

Serves 3 to 4

3 cups fresh basil

³/4 cup grated Parmesan cheese

1/2 cup plus 3 tablespoons olive oil, divided

1/2 cup plus 1/3 cup pine nuts, divided

4 cloves garlic, whole, plus 2 cloves, minced

1 teaspoon salt

1 teaspoon black pepper

2 tablespoons balsamic vinegar

1 cup tomatoes, halved

1/2 red onion, sliced

5 baby bella mushrooms, sliced

4 boneless, skinless chicken breasts

1 1/2 cups quinoa

3 cups chicken broth

1. Preheat oven to 425 degrees.
2. Make balsamic pesto by combining the basil, Parmesan, 1/2 cup olive oil, 1/2 cup pine nuts, 4 whole garlic cloves, salt, pepper, and balsamic vinegar in a food processor. Pulse until smooth.
3. Arrange the tomatoes, red onions, and mushrooms in the base of a 9 x 13-inch baking dish.
4. Arrange chicken breasts on top of vegetables. Spread pesto over chicken. Roast for 30 to 35 minutes.
5. In a medium saucepan bring quinoa, 1/3 cup pine nuts, 3 tablespoons olive oil, chicken broth, and minced garlic to boil over medium heat. Once boiling, cover and reduce to low heat for 15 minutes, or until all liquid is absorbed.
6. Serve chicken and vegetables over quinoa.

APPLE MAC AND GOUDA

This is my version of a classic mac and cheese. I use rigatoni instead of macaroni because it is always so pretty in pasta dishes. I hope the noodle purists of the world will not take exception. (Also, Gouda can be pricey, so partially substituting in a less expensive cheese—like white Cheddar—works well.)

Serves 3 to 4

1 yellow onion, sliced

1 Honeycrisp apple, peeled and cubed

3 tablespoons butter

3 tablespoons whole wheat flour

1 3/4 cups milk

2 1/2 cups grated Gouda cheese, divided

1/2 cup grated Parmesan cheese

1 teaspoon salt

1 teaspoon black pepper

1/4 teaspoon dried thyme

1/4 teaspoon red pepper flakes

1 pound rigatoni, cooked al dente

3 chicken breasts, cooked and shredded

1/3 cup bread crumbs

1. Preheat oven to 350 degrees.
2. In a large skillet heat onion, apple, and butter over medium heat for 5 to 7 minutes, until apples are tender. Stir in flour, cooking for another minute.
3. Increase heat to medium and add milk, 2 cups Gouda, Parmesan, salt, pepper, thyme, and red pepper flakes. Heat for 5 to 7 minutes or until cheese is melted.
4. Toss sauce with noodles and chicken. Transfer to a greased 9 x 13-inch baking dish.
5. Top with reserved Gouda and bread crumbs. Bake for 30 minutes.

SPAGHETTI SQUASH PAD THAI

If you want to back off on grains, using spaghetti squash is a handy substitution for pad thai noodles. I can rarely be convinced to part from my beloved carbohydrates, so I sometimes prepare noodles and still add spaghetti squash for extra texture and nutrients.

Serves 3 to 4

1 spaghetti squash, halved

3 tablespoons soy sauce

1 tablespoon sriracha

2 tablespoons lime juice

2 tablespoons canola oil

2 tablespoons firmly packed light brown sugar

3 chicken breasts, cooked and shredded

2 large eggs, scrambled

1/4 cup bean sprouts

1/4 cup fresh cilantro

3 green onions, sliced

1/4 cup crushed peanuts

1. Preheat oven to 400 degrees.
2. Place spaghetti squash in a glass 9 x 13-inch baking dish. Roast for 40 minutes.
3. Prepare the pad thai sauce by whisking together the soy sauce, sriracha, lime juice, canola oil, and brown sugar.
4. Using a spoon, remove squash from peel.
5. Toss the squash with the chicken, eggs, bean sprouts, cilantro, green onion, and crushed peanuts. Top with pad thai sauce.

CHICKEN NOODLE SOUP

I think my chicken noodle soup is the best I have ever eaten. Maybe that is arrogant to say, or maybe this is the standard we should strive for in our staple recipes—try lots until you find the one your family loves! I like this one for its complexity of flavor and the lovely hint of lemon.

Serves 5 to 6

2 tablespoons butter

1/2 yellow onion, diced

2 cloves garlic, minced

3 carrots, sliced

3 chicken breasts, cooked and shredded

1/2 pound cavatappi noodles

8 cups chicken broth

1 tablespoon lemon juice

1 tablespoon chopped fresh parsley

1/2 teaspoon dried thyme

1/2 teaspoon salt

1 teaspoon black pepper

1/4 teaspoon red pepper flakes

1. Heat the butter, onions, garlic, and carrots in the base of a large pot over medium-low heat for 7 minutes.
2. Increase heat to medium and add chicken breast, cavatappi, chicken broth, lemon juice, parsley, thyme, salt, pepper, and red pepper flakes to pot. Cook for 15 minutes, stirring intermittently.

BARLEY VEGETABLE BOWL

This vegetarian meal is a grain-based salad with barley in place of lettuce. I usually joke with my husband that while I am eating it I can actually feel my cells being nourished. Whenever I have been eating too many sweets I crave a vegetable dish like this and a big glass of water to curb the sugar rush.

Serves 2

1/2 cup barley

1 cup vegetable broth

1 sweet potato, cubed

3 tablespoons water

2 cups broccolini (or broccoli)

2 tablespoons olive oil

Salt to taste

Black pepper to taste

1 avocado, sliced

2 large eggs, hard-boiled and halved

1 cup black beans

Dollop of hummus

Red pepper flakes to taste

Lemon juice to taste

1. Bring barley and vegetable broth to boil in a medium saucepan over high heat. Cover and simmer for 30 minutes.
2. Preheat oven to broil.
3. Microwave sweet potatoes in a shallow dish with 3 tablespoons of water for 3 1/2 minutes. Strain excess water.
4. Toss sweet potatoes and broccolini in olive oil. Season with salt and pepper. Spread sweet potatoes and broccolini onto a parchment paper–lined baking sheet. Broil for 10 minutes.
5. Serve avocado, sweet potatoes, broccolini, and eggs over barley and black beans.
6. Top with hummus. Season with salt, pepper, red pepper flakes, and lemon juice.

SHEPHERD'S PIE CAKES

A standard shepherd's pie is great, but it is so fun to eat these little individual servings. They are cute like cupcakes and hit the spot when you are craving something meaty and filling. Plus, there is something about tiny foods that children have trouble saying no to.

Serves 3 to 4

1 pound ground chuck

1/2 cup peas

2 carrots, diced

1 yellow onion, diced

1 clove garlic, minced

1 large egg

1 tablespoon Worcestershire sauce

1/4 teaspoon dried rosemary

1/2 teaspoon dried thyme

1 teaspoon salt, divided

1 teaspoon black pepper, divided

2 to 3 russet potatoes, cubed

3 tablespoons milk

3 tablespoons butter, cubed

1/4 teaspoon garlic powder

Green onion, sliced

1. Preheat oven to 350 degrees.
2. In a bowl combine ground chuck, peas, carrots, onion, garlic, egg, Worcestershire, rosemary, thyme, 1/2 teaspoon salt, and 1/2 teaspoon pepper.
3. Press meat into cups of a muffin tin and roast for 35 to 40 minutes.
4. Place cubed potatoes in a pot. Cover with water and bring to boil over high heat. Reduce heat to low and simmer for 20 minutes.
5. Place cooked potatoes in bowl of an electric mixer. Blend together on low speed with the milk, butter, 1/2 teaspoon salt, 1/2 teaspoon pepper, and garlic powder, until smooth.
6. Top with the mashed potatoes and green onion.

Happy to Help: A Tip from My Friend
HOW TO CLEAN YOUR GRILL

My friend Heidi's husband, Brad, is a man of many talents. He is a high school English teacher, a father of six (five of whom are boys), an author, and on the side, a blacksmith. Most pertinent to this cookbook's efforts, he is also an at-home grill master.

David and I love grilling, but once the meat is perfectly charred and ready to eat, we are never in the mood to pause and clean the grill grate. What I like about Brad's method for grill cleaning is you can do it before you begin food preparation.

Preheat the grill for ten minutes on the highest setting. Dip a wire brush in water and scrub the grates to create a steam-clean effect. Keep the brush wet while scrubbing. Lingering bits from your last grill will become soft and lift away easily. Decrease the heat to your desired cooking temperature and wipe the grates with a paper towel dipped in oil. (An oil-coated towel will sometimes go up in flames, so it is best to switch it out with a new paper towel often, before it gets too hot).

Brad says, "Do this every time, and it will make the once-a-year deep cleaning a lot easier."

BRAD'S SPATCHCOCK CHICKEN

Here is the masculine contribution to this cookbook, which, of course, is a grilling recipe! This is Brad's go-to recipe for fantastic chicken. If you have ever been scared of grilling a whole bird, this is the perfect way to try it.

Serves 5 to 6

1 (5-pound) whole chicken

3/4 cup lime juice

1/2 cup olive oil

2 tablespoons lime zest

1 tablespoon honey

1 teaspoon salt

1 tablespoon chili powder

2 jalapeño peppers, minced

2 garlic cloves, minced

3 tablespoons fresh cilantro, finely chopped

1. Run a serrated knife along both sides of the backbone of chicken from tail to neck. Remove backbone and make a deep cut from the inside of bird down the middle of breast. Spread open bird and place on a baking sheet.

2. In a bowl combine the lime juice, olive oil, lime zest, honey, salt, chili powder, jalapeños, garlic, and cilantro. Pour over chicken and allow to marinate for 1 hour.

3. Grill over medium heat for about 20 minutes on each side. Baste every 5 to 10 minutes.

4. Allow to rest for 10 minutes before serving.

BLT PIZZA

BLTs and pizza are two American classics. (Well, one is Italian, but we seem to have claimed it.) Put them together and you get this remake of the beloved sandwich in a pleasing pie form.

Makes 3 personal pizzas

1 pound pizza dough

3/4 cup pizza sauce

1 cup grated Asiago (or Parmesan) cheese

10 heirloom medley tomatoes, sliced

1/4 pound bacon, cooked and crumbled

2 cups arugula

1 tablespoon olive oil

1/4 teaspoon salt

1/4 teaspoon black pepper

1. Preheat oven to 450 degrees.
2. Divide pizza dough into 3 even-size balls. Roll out dough about 1/2 inch thick. Place on parchment paper–lined baking sheets.
3. Top with sauce, Asiago, tomatoes, and bacon.
4. Bake for 10 to 12 minutes.
5. In a bowl toss arugula with olive oil, salt, and pepper. Top pizzas with arugula.

BEET AND KALE LASAGNA ROLL-UPS

*I had my first beet at a friend's house when she topped a tasty salad with them.
I was impressed and intrigued, and it inspired me to venture further into beet
territory. They can make a healthy addition to classic comfort foods like lasagna.*

Serves 3 to 4

4 medium beets, peeled and sliced

3 tablespoons olive oil, divided

1/2 teaspoon salt

1/2 teaspoon black pepper

8 kale leaves, de-stemmed and sliced

Pinch of ground nutmeg

Pinch of red pepper flakes

1 cup ricotta cheese

1 teaspoon Italian Seasoning
(recipe on page 160)

1 large egg

6 lasagna noodles, cooked al dente

3/4 pound bacon, cooked and crumbled

1 cup shredded mozzarella cheese

1. Preheat oven to 450 degrees.
2. Arrange beets on a parchment paper–lined baking sheet. Drizzle with 1 tablespoon olive oil and season with salt and pepper. Roast for 30 minutes.
3. Reduce oven heat to 350 degrees.
4. Heat 2 tablespoons olive oil in a large skillet over medium heat. Sauté kale and season with nutmeg and red pepper flakes. Once kale is wilted and soft, set aside.
5. Puree the roasted beets in a food processor. If the beet puree is not creamy, add a teaspoon of olive oil and puree until smooth.
6. In a bowl stir together the ricotta, Italian seasoning, and egg.
7. Spread ricotta mixture onto individual lasagna noodles. Layer with the beet puree, bacon, and kale.
8. Roll noodle into a spiral and arrange in a greased 1 1/2-quart baking dish. Top with mozzarella.
9. Bake lasagna for 30 minutes.

HAM AND SWISS HAND PIES

There is something wonderful about having a warm pie full of fabulous ingredients in handheld form. Somehow it makes those ingredients taste even better. My family loves this take on the old ham and Swiss classic.

Makes 6 mini pies

¹/₄ cup Dijon mustard

¹/₂ teaspoon honey

1 teaspoon black pepper

2 sheets piecrust

12 slices ham

¹/₂ yellow onion, sliced and caramelized

6 slices Swiss cheese

1 large egg

1 tablespoon water

1. Preheat oven to 450 degrees.
2. In a small bowl whisk together Dijon, honey, and pepper.
3. Evenly roll out piecrust to ¹/₈-inch thickness. Using a 4-inch pastry cutter, cut 12 circles out of piecrust.
4. Layer 2 slices of ham, onion, and Swiss cheese onto a layer of piecrust. Spread Dijon sauce on top of Swiss. Top with second layer of piecrust.
5. Seal edges with fork. Arrange the pies on a parchment paper–lined baking sheet.
6. Whisk together egg and 1 tablespoon of water. Brush egg wash over pies.
7. Bake for 11 to 13 minutes.

PLUM CAPRESE STUFFED PORK LOIN

In my humble opinion, caprese is genius—it is just a perfectly balanced combination of flavors. I hope to make the inventor proud by creating this version with sautéed plums. It is hard to go wrong with just about any form of caprese.

Serves 3 to 4

1 pound pork loin roast

1 yellow onion, sliced

1 tablespoon olive oil

Salt to taste

Black pepper to taste

2 plums, diced (or 8 ounces canned plums)

5 basil leaves

1/2 cup mozzarella pearls

Kitchen twine

1. Preheat oven to 450 degrees.
2. Cut pork loin vertically down the center about 2/3 through (enough to make room for stuffing).
3. In a large skillet over medium heat, sauté onion with olive oil, salt, and pepper for 10 minutes. Add the plum and continue to cook for 3 minutes.
4. Stuff basil leaves into pork loin. Layer in the plums and onion. Top with mozzarella pearls. Season with salt and pepper. Tie pork loin closed with twine. Transfer pork loin to parchment paper-lined baking sheet.
5. Roast for 60 minutes.

BUTTERNUT SQUASH GOULASH

*The sweetness of butternut squash mingled with the savory zing of smoked sausage
makes this dish pop. Butternut squash is a fantastic ingredient. Although it is at
its prime in autumn, I love to cook with it as often as I can throughout the year.*

Serves 4

1 butternut squash

1/2 yellow onion, sliced

3 tablespoons butter

3/4 pound smoked sausage, sliced

3 cloves garlic, minced

1 cup vegetable broth

1 tablespoon Dijon mustard

1 teaspoon salt

1 teaspoon black pepper

1 tablespoon Italian Seasoning
(recipe on page 160)

1/4 teaspoon paprika

1/2 pound rotini pasta, cooked al dente

1/4 cup grated Parmesan cheese

1. Preheat oven to 350 degrees.
2. Slice butternut squash in half. Remove seeds and place facedown in a glass baking dish. Roast for 45 minutes.
3. Sauté onion in a large skillet with butter over medium heat for 5 to 7 minutes, until tender. Add the sausage and garlic, cooking until browned.
4. Puree the butternut squash in a food processor with the vegetable broth and Dijon.
5. In a bowl combine onion-and-sausage mixture with butternut squash puree. Season with the salt, pepper, Italian seasoning, and paprika.
6. Toss with noodles and top with Parmesan.

LOADED BAKED POTATO GNOCCHI

Gnocchi is like a fluffy potato-based pasta. The words fluffy and potato-based always get my attention. This version of gnocchi is kind of the only gnocchi in my book. If you love baked potatoes, you just have to try them in this form.

Serves 3 to 4

5 cups water

1 1/2 pounds potato gnocchi

2 tablespoons butter

1 clove garlic, minced

3/4 pound bacon, cooked and crumbled

1 cup shredded Cheddar cheese

2 teaspoons chives, sliced

3 green onions, sliced

Salt to taste

Black pepper to taste

1. Bring 5 cups water to boil in a large saucepan over medium-high heat. Place gnocchi into water and cook for 2 minutes, stirring occasionally, until al dente. Strain gnocchi and set aside.

2. In a large skillet melt butter over medium heat. Add the gnocchi and brown in butter for 8 minutes. Add garlic and cook for an additional 2 minutes.

3. Remove from skillet and top gnocchi with the bacon, Cheddar, chives, green onions, salt, and pepper.

SIDES, SAUCES, AND SEASONINGS

Raspberry Basil Whipped Butter

Walnut Pesto

Blue Cheese Sauce

Apple and Parmesan Coleslaw

Pomegranate Wheat Berry Salad

Greek Pasta Salad

Bethany's Blanched Vegetable Medley

Roasted Asparagus

Greek Seasoning

Mexican Seasoning

Italian Seasoning

Cajun Seasoning

Salsa

Roasted Vegetable Guacamole

Stefan's Bacon Jalapeño Mac and Cheese

Broccoli and Cauliflower Tots

Grandma's Cucumber Salad

Carrot and Parsnip Fries

Mashed Potato Casserole

White Cheddar Croutons

SWITCHING SIDES

We have all been in the weeknight dinner rut. I was there for quite a while a few years ago. Whenever I tried to decide what to cook, I felt completely uninspired. Usually we resigned to eating the same few meals over and over again.

Besides the repetition, another problem with our dinners was they were very basic. When I say "basic," I am not saying simple food is bad or that every night we should strive to prepare a rack of lamb. I just mean our meals needed a little more spark. We discovered that adding just one easy, different element to a meal could make it feel like something brand-new. What brought a breakthrough for me was putting more thought into the side dishes—changing them up and playing with new ingredients.

This idea does not require much more planning, or even work. I used to make a variation of the same pasta, red sauce, and meat about once a week. Eventually we started to hate eating it and dreaded cooking dinner altogether. (My husband loves this meal, but I kind of overdid it.) Instead, I now repeat some things week in and week out (like chicken breasts with our favorite marinade), but I add variety with the other courses. And more of them! You can make chicken and green beans every week and get completely bored. Or you can pair the same chicken with a variety of sides, and it feels like a fresh meal every time. Grilled chicken with a yellow pepper pesto and dinner rolls feels totally different from the same chicken with grilled corn and a green salad. If the people you are cooking for are anything like my husband, they will love getting to feel more full at dinner from bonus sides.

Having fun with sides can take the pressure off in the menu-planning department. You can stick with a few tried-and-true entrées and find inspiration for the rest from what is in season, or from a recipe or food photo that piques your interest. Do your best with whatever is available to you—whether it is at the market, in your garden, or already in your pantry.

And certainly invite people over to savor your creations with you. Remember you do not need to create anything fancy to impress; friends feel welcome by the warmth of your conversation more than a magazine-worthy, gourmet spread. What we aim for is not polish and grandeur, but lovingly and thoughtfully being faithful with what we have been given.

RASPBERRY BASIL WHIPPED BUTTER

Butter is an absolute blessing all by itself, but it can be dressed up easily when you need something extra special to take a dish to a new level. A butter this spruced makes even the plainest breads look fancy.

Makes 1 cup

¼ cup raspberries

¼ teaspoon sugar

1 teaspoon vanilla extract

1 cup (2 sticks) butter, softened

5 basil leaves, sliced

1. Using a whisk attachment, combine raspberries, sugar, and vanilla with an electric mixer on medium speed for 1 minute.
2. Add butter and continue to mix for 2 to 3 minutes, until combined throughout. Fold in basil.

WALNUT PESTO

I love eating fresh pesto, but the price of pine nuts used in traditional pesto is outrageous. I usually make this walnut adaptation because it has an equally nice nuttiness at a much lower cost. Pesto is beloved when tossed with pasta, but I recommend also smearing it on bread, drizzling it over meat, and stirring it into salad dressings.

Makes 2 cups

4 cups fresh basil

1 cup grated Parmesan cheese

1 ¼ cup olive oil

²/3 cup walnuts

6 cloves garlic

1 teaspoon salt

1 teaspoon black pepper

1. Pulse the basil, Parmesan, olive oil, walnuts, garlic, salt, and pepper together in a food processor until smooth.

BLUE CHEESE SAUCE

A turning point in our marriage was when my husband started liking blue cheese. (Don't scientists say if you eat a food enough times you will like it?) Now he loves it more than I do! Enjoy this creamy, salty sauce on sandwiches, vegetables, steaks, fries, or pizza.

Makes about 2 cups

2 tablespoons butter, melted

1/2 cup milk

5 ounces blue cheese

1/2 teaspoon red pepper flakes

1/2 teaspoon salt

1 teaspoon black pepper

2 teaspoons lemon juice

2 tablespoons olive oil

1/2 avocado

2 tablespoons chives

1. Blend together the butter, milk, blue cheese, red pepper flakes, salt, pepper, lemon juice, olive oil, and avocado in a food processor until smooth.
2. Fold chives into sauce.

APPLE AND PARMESAN COLESLAW

If you are averse to regular coleslaw, I have a feeling you will consider this olive oil rendition a pleasure. Somehow julienning fruits and vegetables— slicing into long, thin strips—always seems to make them taste even better.

Serves 5 to 6

1 head of cabbage, shredded

1 carrot, julienned

1 red onion, julienned

1 apple, julienned

3 teaspoons Dijon mustard

3 tablespoons honey

1/2 cup olive oil

3 tablespoons apple cider vinegar

1/4 cup lime juice

1 1/2 teaspoons garlic powder

1/2 teaspoon salt

1/2 teaspoon black pepper

3 tablespoons Parmesan cheese, grated

1. In a large bowl stir together the cabbage, carrot, red onion, and apple.

2. In a small bowl whisk together the Dijon, honey, olive oil, apple cider vinegar, lime juice, garlic powder, salt, and pepper.

3. Toss cabbage mixture with dressing. Chill for at least an hour. Top with Parmesan.

POMEGRANATE WHEAT BERRY SALAD

Finding another creative way to serve a flavorful salad is always a victory. It takes some time to get those little pomegranate jewels out of their caves, but once they are liberated, you have the key ingredient to a healthy recipe that wows. Most grocery stores now sell pomegranate seeds in cups in the cold area of the produce section too.

Serves 2

1/2 cup wheat berries (or quinoa, barley, or rice)

1 1/2 cups water

1/4 pound bacon, cooked and crumbled

1 pomegranate, seeded

4 cups mixed field greens

1/4 cup pine nuts

2 tablespoons lemon juice

2 tablespoons balsamic vinegar

1/4 cup olive oil

1/2 teaspoon black pepper

2 teaspoons honey

1. Bring wheat berries and 1 1/2 cups of water in a small saucepan to a boil over high heat. Reduce heat to low. Cover and simmer for 20 minutes until wheat berries are tender. Drain any excess water.
2. Combine the wheat berries, bacon, pomegranate seeds, mixed greens, and pine nuts in a large bowl.
3. In a separate bowl whisk together the lemon juice, vinegar, olive oil, pepper, and honey.
4. Toss salad with dressing.

GREEK PASTA SALAD

*If you plan on attending a picnic, cookout, or potluck in the summer, you
need to have a fabulous pasta salad recipe up your sleeve. This fresh
summer Greek pasta salad would be a winner at any get-together.*

Serves 3 to 4

2 tablespoons balsamic vinegar

1 teaspoon sugar

2 cloves garlic, minced

3 tablespoons plus 1/4 cup olive oil, divided

1 pound boneless, skinless chicken breasts

12 ounces angel hair pasta, cooked al dente

1 pint cherry tomatoes, halved

1 red onion, diced

1/2 cup crumbled feta cheese

1 cucumber, sliced

1 orange bell pepper, diced

3 tablespoons red wine vinegar

3 tablespoons lemon juice

1 tablespoon Dijon mustard

1 tablespoon honey

1 teaspoon dried oregano

1 teaspoon dried parsley

1/2 teaspoon salt

1/2 teaspoon black pepper

1. In a small bowl whisk together balsamic vinegar, sugar, garlic, and 3 tablespoons olive oil. Marinate the chicken in mixture for 2 to 8 hours, or overnight.

2. Preheat oven to 450 degrees. Place chicken in a baking pan and roast for 30 minutes, flipping halfway through.

3. Slice cooked chicken and toss in a large bowl with the pasta, tomatoes, onion, feta, cucumber, and bell pepper.

4. In a small bowl whisk together 1/4 cup olive oil, red wine vinegar, lemon juice, Dijon, honey, oregano, parsley, salt, and pepper.

5. Toss salad in dressing.

Happy to Help: A Tip from My Friend

PREPARING DINNER IN THE MORNING

My friend Bethany jokes that the hours from 4:00 to 6:00 p.m. in her house are awful. "My kids are tired, everyone's blood sugar is low, and I am ready to clock out. I find as my desire to be 'done' with mothering for the day grows, so does my children's need to be cared for," she says. Seeing Bethany's life, I have learned how a hardworking mom can bring peace and provision even in the low moments.

One way to curb the horror of the late-afternoon witching hour is making dinner preparations early in the day while kids are occupied with other tasks or sleeping. Bethany is always experimenting with what can be premade and still look and taste great. You can marinate meat, dice vegetables, or assemble salads. She adds, "Spaghetti sauce cooks slowly all day. Homemade pizzas refrigerate well. You can bread chicken tenders and quickly pan-fry them later. Or try prebaking chicken breasts and finishing them on the grill."

Slow cookers are of course nice for some things, but Bethany has convinced me that morning dinner preparation can simplify many of our dinner menus.

BETHANY'S BLANCHED VEGETABLE MEDLEY

Vegetables are often underappreciated because they are not prepared well. Bethany is really not a fan of the overcooked and discolored ones, so she has mastered this technique, which results in bright, perfectly cooked veggies every time.

Serves 3 to 4

1 1/4 tablespoons salt, divided

20 sugar snap peas

1/2 head cauliflower, chopped into florets

4 carrots, peeled and sliced

5 asparagus stems, sliced into thirds

2 tablespoons olive oil

6 baby bella mushrooms, sliced

2 mint leaves, chopped

1/4 teaspoon garlic powder

1/4 teaspoon black pepper

1. Fill a large skillet halfway with water and 1 tablespoon of salt and bring to a boil.
2. Prepare an ice bath by filling a large bowl with ice and cold water. Place sugar snap peas in boiling water for 30 seconds. Remove from water and transfer to ice bath.
3. Place cauliflower in boiling water for 3 to 4 minutes. Remove from water and transfer to ice bath.
4. Place carrots in boiling water for 5 minutes. Remove from water and transfer to ice bath.
5. Place asparagus in boiling water for 2 minutes. Remove from water and transfer to ice bath.
6. Empty skillet of water and drizzle with olive oil. Strain vegetables from ice bath and add to skillet with mushrooms. Cook for 2 to 3 minutes over medium heat, until warm.
7. Season with mint, garlic powder, remaining 1/4 teaspoon salt, and pepper.

ROASTED ASPARAGUS

For years we rarely ate asparagus because I always sautéed it, and that never quite got the tough, raw flavor out of the stalks. I usually ended up eating only the flavorful tips. Then my best friend, Elysia, taught me to roast asparagus, which is so uncomplicated and gives the final product a much nicer consistency.

Serves 3 to 4

1 bundle asparagus

2 tablespoons olive oil

2 cloves garlic, minced

1 teaspoon balsamic vinegar

Salt to taste

Black pepper to taste

¼ cup shredded Parmesan cheese

1. Preheat oven to 450 degrees.
2. In a glass 9 x 13-inch baking dish, toss asparagus with olive oil, garlic, and balsamic vinegar. Season with salt and pepper.
3. Roast for 25 to 30 minutes.
4. Top with shredded Parmesan.

GREEK SEASONING

*Try this on feta, gyros, a Greek salad, or anything else that needs a little dash of
savory flavor. I put it in a soup for David once, and one of his coworkers demanded
to know the recipe of whatever seasoning could make such a delicious aroma.*

Makes about 10 servings of 3 tablespoons

1/2 cup dried basil

1/2 cup dried oregano

1/3 cup dried parsley

1/4 cup garlic powder

1/4 cup dried thyme

3 tablespoons black pepper

2 tablespoons salt

1 teaspoon ground cinnamon

1. Mix together the basil, oregano, parsley,
   garlic powder, thyme, pepper, salt,
   and cinnamon, and store in an airtight
   container.

MEXICAN SEASONING

Mexican food is fantastic; everyone knows this. The store-bought Mexican seasoning, however, is underwhelming. The iridescent orange color, the billion ingredients, and the high sodium content convinced me to develop a homemade version.

Makes about 10 servings of 3 tablespoons

1 cup chili powder

¼ cup paprika

3 tablespoons onion powder

2 tablespoons garlic powder

2 tablespoons salt

1 tablespoon red pepper flakes

1 tablespoon dried oregano

1 tablespoon black pepper

1. Mix together the chili powder, paprika, onion powder, garlic powder, salt, red pepper flakes, oregano, and black pepper, and store in an airtight container.

ITALIAN SEASONING

I use this seasoning often because it is the right complement for any of the "red sauce" meals—like pizza and pasta dishes. Throw this seasoning on any and all of them. I also make a dipping sauce for bread by mixing 1 tablespoon of this seasoning with 1/4 cup of olive oil.

Makes about 10 servings of 3 tablespoons

3/4 cup dried basil

3/4 cup dried oregano

1/3 cup dried thyme

3 tablespoons garlic powder

2 tablespoons salt

1 teaspoon red pepper flakes

1. Mix together the basil, oregano, thyme, garlic powder, salt, and red pepper flakes, and store in an airtight container.

160

CAJUN SEASONING

I cannot afford a trip to the Bayou whenever I am looking for good Cajun food. I can afford to combine these simple spices to bring a taste of Louisiana to our table. Add this seasoning to shrimp or sausage dishes along with red beans and rice for an easy change of pace.

Makes about 10 servings of 3 tablespoons

3/4 cup paprika

3 tablespoons cumin

3 tablespoons garlic powder

1/3 cup dried oregano

3 tablespoons salt

3 tablespoons black pepper

2 teaspoons red pepper flakes

1. Mix together the paprika, cumin, garlic powder, oregano, salt, black pepper, and red pepper flakes, and store in an airtight container.

SALSA

I like my salsa very smooth, a little sweet, and not too spicy. I have grown attached to making my own at home because I can get it fresh and exactly how I like it. People love combining salsa with all kinds of things—omelets, tacos, even French fries. For a chunkier version, you can chop the tomatoes, onion, and jalapeño to your desired size instead of blending them.

Makes about 2 cups

1 (14-ounce) can whole tomatoes with juice

1 pint grape tomatoes

1/2 white onion

2 cloves garlic

1 jalapeño pepper

1 tablespoon honey

1/4 cup fresh cilantro

1 lime, juice

1/2 teaspoon Mexican Seasoning (recipe on page 158)

1 teaspoon salt

1. Pulse the whole tomatoes with juice, grape tomatoes, onion, garlic, jalapeño, honey, cilantro, lime juice, Mexican seasoning, and salt in a food processor until smooth, or desired consistency. Serve with tortilla chips.

ROASTED VEGETABLE GUACAMOLE

I may make some enemies by confessing this, but sometimes I find plain guacamole bland. These roasted vegetables perk up the taste with a little added complexity.

Serves 3 to 4

3 shallots, diced

4 baby bella mushrooms, diced

1/2 orange bell pepper, sliced

1/2 cup grape tomatoes, quartered

2 teaspoons olive oil

1/2 teaspoon salt

1/4 teaspoon black pepper

3 avocados

2 tablespoons lemon juice

1 tablespoon fresh parsley, chopped

1. Preheat oven to 400 degrees.
2. In a bowl toss shallots, mushrooms, bell peppers, and tomatoes with the olive oil, salt, and pepper.
3. Place on a baking sheet and roast for 30 minutes.
4. In a bowl mash avocados with lemon juice and parsley.
5. Mix avocado with roasted vegetables.

Happy to Help: A Tip from My Friend

COOKING WITH BACON FAT

Stefan and her husband, Josh, are one of our favorite couples to stay up late with, getting into good, long conversations. I have yet to have a dinner at her house where she cut corners on the meal. (How does she do it? One day she will have to crack!) Her table is always full of a variety of made-from-scratch courses and a creative dessert.

I think her very best dish might be her macaroni, which I had to get her to share here. When I pressed her for what makes it so exceptional, she decreed, "Always save the bacon fat when frying bacon!" To do this, we put it in a glass jar and stash it in the freezer.

Coating a freshly strained batch of pasta with a tablespoon or two of the stuff keeps the noodles from sticking (perfect for preparing pasta in advance) and adds a subtle smoky undertone. The same secret ingredient can add an extra dimension of flavor when sautéing chicken and vegetables too. A particular favorite of Stefan's children is pancakes cooked in bacon fat. I welcome even more ways we can love bacon!

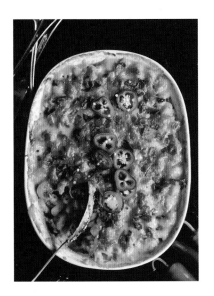

STEFAN'S BACON JALAPEÑO MAC AND CHEESE

Sometimes picking a random cheese to buy in the grocery store can pay off with a happy discovery. This is how Stefan learned that the hearty and smooth Pinconning cheese is an ideal choice for macaroni dishes. Her other smart tip is to use large noodles, like cavatappi, for cheesy pastas. Everyone will thank you for serving this.

Serves 3 to 4

6 tablespoons butter

1/2 cup all-purpose flour

2 teaspoons salt

1 1/2 teaspoons mustard powder

1/2 teaspoon black pepper

5 cups milk

6 cups Pinconning cheese, divided (Colby Jack works too)

1 pound bacon, cooked and crumbled

1 jalapeño pepper, diced

1 pound cavatappi pasta, cooked al dente

1 to 2 tablespoons bacon fat (optional)

1. Preheat oven to 375 degrees.
2. In a large saucepan over medium heat, melt butter. Add the flour, salt, mustard powder, and pepper. Stir constantly for 2 to 3 minutes.
3. Add milk and whisk for 10 minutes. Remove from heat and stir in 4 1/2 cups cheese until melted.
4. Fold in the bacon and jalapeño, reserving 1 cup for topping.
5. Optional: Toss cooked cavatappi in bacon fat.
6. Pour cheese sauce over pasta and toss to coat.
7. Transfer pasta to a 2-quart baking dish. Top with reserved cheese, bacon, and jalapeños.
8. Bake for 25 to 30 minutes.

BROCCOLI AND CAULIFLOWER TOTS

I was never a fan of school cafeteria or frozen tater tots. They did not seem anything like the potatoes they allegedly came from! These are undoubtedly more nutritious and also much more flavorful.

Makes about 30 tots

2 cups broccoli, steamed

2 cups cauliflower, steamed

2 large eggs

1/2 yellow onion

2 cloves garlic

1 cup shredded mozzarella cheese

1/4 cup grated Parmesan cheese

1 teaspoon Italian Seasoning (recipe on page 160)

1/2 teaspoon salt

1/2 teaspoon black pepper

1 cup bread crumbs, plus extra for breading

1. Preheat oven to 400 degrees.
2. Place the broccoli, cauliflower, eggs, onion, garlic, mozzarella, Parmesan, Italian seasoning, salt, and pepper in a food processor. Pulse until no chunks remain.
3. Transfer vegetable mixture to a bowl. Fold in 1 cup bread crumbs. Shape into 1-inch, oval-shaped tots. (To speed things up you can form an easier rectangle or round shape.)
4. Roll tots in additional bread crumbs. Arrange on a parchment paper–lined baking sheet.
5. Bake for 25 to 30 minutes, until golden.

GRANDMA'S CUCUMBER SALAD

My husband, David, considers this recipe to be one of the greatest gifts his grandma has ever given him. If he finds a cucumber in the house, it will end up in this salad. Try it out as a topping on burgers.

Serves 3 to 4

1/4 cup salt

6 cups water

2 cucumbers, sliced thinly

1/4 yellow onion, sliced

2/3 cup apple cider vinegar

1/4 cup sugar

1/2 teaspoon dill

1. In a large bowl mix together salt and 6 cups water until dissolved. Place the cucumbers in water and let soak for 30 minutes. Drain water.
2. Stir the onion, apple cider vinegar, sugar, and dill into the cucumbers.

CARROT AND PARSNIP FRIES

Make no mistake, I am not above enjoying the standard, favorite-of-the-masses French fry. But when the family could use a little variety, I throw them this spiced root version.

Serves 3 to 4

8 carrots, peeled and sliced

2 parsnips, peeled and sliced

1/4 cup olive oil

1/2 teaspoon firmly packed light brown sugar

1/2 teaspoon salt

1 teaspoon black pepper

1 teaspoon onion powder

1 teaspoon chili powder

1 tablespoon crumbled feta

1 teaspoon chives, chopped

1. Preheat oven to 450 degrees.
2. In a bowl toss carrots and parsnips in the olive oil, brown sugar, salt, pepper, onion powder, and chili powder.
3. Arrange on a baking sheet and bake for 30 to 35 minutes.
4. Top with feta and chives.

MASHED POTATO CASSEROLE

This crowd-pleaser can be prepared in advance, which makes it ideal for entertaining. Sometimes I playfully refer to casserole dishes as "cassies." This one evolved into "mashed cassie," "mash cass," or even "masherole." I know, I have gone too far, but I love this side dish that can also fill in as dinner.

Serves 5 to 6

5 russet potatoes, cubed

1/3 cup milk

6 tablespoons butter, cubed

1 teaspoon salt

1 teaspoon black pepper

1/2 teaspoon garlic powder

1/4 cup grated Parmesan cheese

1 pound bacon, cooked and crumbled, divided

1 1/2 cups shredded Cheddar cheese

5 green onions, sliced

1. Place cubed potatoes in a pot. Cover with water and bring to boil over high heat. Reduce heat to low and simmer for 20 minutes.
2. Preheat oven to 350 degrees.
3. Place cooked potatoes in bowl of an electric mixer. Blend together on low speed with the milk, butter, salt, pepper, garlic powder, Parmesan, and 1/4 of the bacon until smooth.
4. Spread potatoes into a 9 x 13-inch baking dish. Top with Cheddar and remaining bacon. Bake for 15 minutes.
5. Top with green onions.

WHITE CHEDDAR CROUTONS

If I buy croutons at the store, they are usually treated like a snack and eaten by the handful before they ever touch a salad. These croutons are too delicious to suffer such a fate. I save them to dress up my special soups and salads.

Makes about 40 croutons

1 loaf Italian bread, sliced into cubes

½ cup olive oil

½ teaspoon black pepper

1 cup shredded white Cheddar cheese

1. Preheat oven to 350 degrees.
2. Place bread in a bowl and toss with olive oil and pepper.
3. Arrange bread on a parchment paper-lined baking sheet and bake for 12 to 13 minutes.
4. Flip croutons and sprinkle with white Cheddar. Bake for 5 more minutes.

DESSERTS

Cinnamon Toast Cereal Cupcakes

Cherry Cake Bars

Chocolate Lasagna

Coconut Lemon Bars

Candy Bar Cookies

Blood Orange Upside-Down Cake

Apple Cinnamon Crisp Rice Treats

Nanny's Rice Pudding

Greta's Peanut Butter Fudge

White Chocolate Twice-Baked Sweet Potatoes

Coconut Macaroons

S'more Cupcakes

Cocoa and Zucchini Strawberry Shortcake

Banana Cake

Doughnut Milkshake

Strawberry Lemon Sorbet

Danielle's No-Bake Cookies

Chocolate Frosting

Vanilla Frosting

Peanut Butter Frosting

Strawberry Frosting

Cream Cheese Frosting

Peppermint Frosting

Neapolitan Smoothie

Sugar-Roasted Slow Cooker Almonds

A LOVE LETTER TO SEASONAL EATING

Whenever I am asked what my favorite season is, I feel an ache of tension in my heart. Choose *one*? How could I? I used to settle for saying my favorite was whichever one was approaching next. Eventually I discovered a more accurate way to describe how I feel. Rather than having a preferred season, I just love that there *are* seasons—that the world was made with these four ebbs and flows, each with its own personality. And unquestionably, much of what makes seasons what they are has to do with food. What we eat tightly intertwines with the richness of each month. (And I have saved myself a lot of trouble by working with the calendar instead of against it when choosing produce for our meals.)

To me, the edible pieces of each time of year help define the season's character. I think it is nearly impossible to be in a sour mood if it is late spring and you are cranking up the grill for the first time in months. The open flame flavors the meat in a way the dry roast of an oven could not all winter. Standing on the porch, breathing in the warm outdoor air we have not felt for so long, it is like our bodies are freshly waking up from sleep.

Then the heat of summer comes, and everything is hot and saturated. The freshness of vegetables is delectable. (I can scarcely eat a carrot in the winter if I linger too long remembering what they really taste like in summer.) Life moves outdoors. The trees in our yard are fully leaved, creating a hidden spot for us to walk on bouncy grass while eating Popsicles, or to cuddle up in sweatshirts at night and eat roasted marshmallows.

It would be sad when the summer ended if it were not for the treasures of fall that come after it. I think the world feels closest to what heaven will be like in autumn. We work, then harvest. Toil, then rest. The skies get moodier, but the air is still crisp. The hustle and bustle of school rolls in, punctuated with swirls of nutmeg and pumpkin. It seems as though everyone is more careful in fall—more mindful. We know the colder months are coming, so we savor a late night spent sitting on the porch or that last walk around the block without a coat.

David and I joke that Christmas is its own fifth season that lasts the month of December, distinct from the rest of winter. Children seem their most wide-eyed and in awe at this time. Here in Michigan, when we do not have snow on Christmas, my entire year feels off balance while I wait for the next December to put it back in place again. Barely two nights can pass without my making another baked treat to eat by the tree's light while we watch our next movie together.

I will never tire of the seasons' sweet abundance and how God is making Himself plain through it. Before I can miss any one of them too much, I am overcome with the thrill of the next one arriving.

CINNAMON TOAST CEREAL CUPCAKES

Some have told me these are the best cupcakes they have ever eaten.
Most people love the sweet-milk leftover after a bowl of sugary cereal, and
these were the result of experimenting with that flavorful milk in baking.
Also, I kind of endeavor to insert cereal into every part of the day.

Makes 12 cupcakes

2 cups cinnamon toast cereal, divided

1 cup milk

$1/2$ cup (1 stick) butter, softened

1 cup sugar

1 large egg

1 $3/4$ cups all-purpose flour

$3/4$ teaspoon baking powder

$1/2$ teaspoon salt

$1/2$ teaspoon ground nutmeg

1 teaspoon ground cinnamon

$1/2$ teaspoon baking soda

Vanilla Frosting (recipe on page 220)

1. Preheat oven to 350 degrees.
2. Steep 1 cup of cereal in milk for 15 minutes.
3. Mix together butter, sugar, and egg with an electric mixer on medium-low speed for 1 to 2 minutes.
4. In a separate bowl combine flour, baking powder, salt, nutmeg, cinnamon, and baking soda.
5. Remove cereal from milk and discard. Slowly incorporate flour mixture and cereal milk into butter mixture.
6. Divide batter into a paper cup–lined muffin tin, filling each cup about $2/3$ full. Bake for 20 minutes.
7. Pulse remaining 1 cup cereal in a food processor and stir crumbs into vanilla frosting. Allow cupcakes to cool, and then frost.

CHERRY CAKE BARS

Everyone loves this super easy dessert that my family calls "Cherries Jubilee." We know that is not what it actually is, but it is just too fun a phrase to resist. If you must, "Cherry Cake Bars" will do!

Makes about 20 bars

3/4 cup (1 1/2 sticks) butter, softened

2 1/4 cups sugar

6 large eggs

4 1/2 cups all-purpose flour

2 1/4 teaspoons baking powder

1 1/2 teaspoons salt

1 1/2 teaspoons vanilla extract

2 (21-ounce) cans cherry pie filling

1. Preheat oven to 350 degrees.
2. Using an electric mixer cream together butter and sugar on medium-low speed for 1 to 2 minutes. Add the eggs, flour, baking powder, salt, and vanilla. Continue to mix until combined, about 2 minutes.
3. Press 2/3 batter into a greased, rimmed baking sheet. Spread into an even layer.
4. Pour cherry pie filling over top. Drop remaining batter onto the pie filling.
5. Bake for 40 minutes. Allow to cool.

CHOCOLATE LASAGNA

The title might sound a little peculiar, but this dessert has nothing to do with meat and cheese. Think layered, milky chocolate goodness. I like desserts with lots of different textures, and a big, multilayered lasagna was the perfect inspiration for a sweet version. I am out of bounds and loving it.

Serves 12

Brownies (prepared in 9 x 13-inch glass baking dish)

3 cups chocolate pudding

1 cup heavy cream

1/2 teaspoon vanilla extract

2 tablespoons powdered sugar

20 chocolate sandwich cookies, crushed

1. Prepare brownies and allow to cool.
2. Prepare pudding according to package directions. Spread pudding over brownies, then cover and refrigerate 8 to 12 hours, or overnight.
3. The next day whisk heavy cream with an electric mixer on high for 4 to 5 minutes until cream thickens. Stir in vanilla and powdered sugar.
4. Layer whipped cream on top of pudding.
5. Top with crushed chocolate sandwich cookies.

COCONUT LEMON BARS

This treat is a huge hit with the gluten-free crowd. You always have to find a way to keep gluten-free desserts from getting too dry, and the lovely lemon filling here keeps everything delicious and gooey.

Makes 9 bars

1 cup coconut flour

1/2 cup sweetened shredded coconut, plus extra for topping

1/4 cup sugar

1/3 cup coconut oil, melted

2 large eggs

1/4 cup lemon juice

1/2 cup sugar

2 tablespoons cornstarch

1. Preheat oven to 350 degrees.
2. In a bowl stir together the coconut flour, shredded coconut, sugar, and coconut oil. Press crust into a 9 x 9-inch baking pan. Bake for 10 minutes.
3. In a separate bowl whisk the eggs. Continue whisking while adding lemon juice, sugar, and cornstarch.
4. Pour onto cooled crust and bake 18 to 20 minutes.
5. Top with additional shredded coconut.

CANDY BAR COOKIES

Chocolate-covered pretzels are my spirit animal. Any candy bar or dessert that includes them is a hit with me, and these candy bar cookies are one of them. There is something about a fresh batch of homemade cookies that a convenience store candy bar just cannot offer.

Makes 24 cookies

1/2 cup (1 stick) butter, softened

1 cup peanut butter

1/4 cup sugar

3/4 cup firmly packed light brown sugar

1 large egg

1 tablespoon vanilla extract

1 teaspoon baking soda

1 teaspoon salt

1 1/2 cups all-purpose flour

1 cup caramel apple dip

1/4 cup peanuts, chopped

2 cups chocolate chips

24 pretzels

1. Preheat oven to 350 degrees.
2. In the bowl of an electric mixer combine the butter, peanut butter, sugar, and brown sugar on medium-low speed for 1 to 2 minutes. Add the egg and vanilla, continuing to mix until combined, about 2 minutes.
3. In a separate bowl stir together the baking soda, salt, and flour. Slowly incorporate flour mixture into butter mixture until ingredients are combined.
4. Shape into 1 1/2-inch balls and arrange on a parchment paper–lined baking sheet. Slightly flatten each ball of dough with a fork. Bake 8 to 9 minutes.
5. Allow to cool. Spread a layer of caramel on top of each cookie. Sprinkle with chopped peanuts.
6. Place chocolate chips in a microwavable bowl. Microwave on low until smooth, pausing to stir every 30 seconds.
7. Spread melted chocolate over peanuts and top with pretzels. Allow the cookies to cool.

BLOOD ORANGE UPSIDE-DOWN CAKE

This is a beautiful cake for a special gathering. Because it uses honey and orange juice to replace some of the white sugar, it has an extremely moist texture and rich flavor palette.

Serves 8 to 10

1/2 cup (1 stick) butter, melted, plus 1 cup (2 sticks) butter, softened

1/2 cup honey

3 blood oranges, peeled and sliced (any seasonal orange works too!)

2/3 cup firmly packed light brown sugar

1/2 cup sugar

2 large eggs

1 1/2 cups all-purpose flour

3/4 teaspoon baking powder

1/2 teaspoon baking soda

1/2 teaspoon salt

1 1/4 cups orange juice

1 teaspoon orange zest

1. Preheat oven to 350 degrees.
2. In a small bowl stir together melted butter and honey. Pour into bottom of a greased Bundt pan. Place sliced oranges in butter and honey mixture in a single layer around pan.
3. With an electric mixer beat together the softened butter, brown sugar, and sugar on medium-low speed for 1 to 2 minutes. Add eggs and mix until combined.
4. In a separate bowl stir together the flour, baking powder, baking soda, and salt. Slowly incorporate flour mixture and orange juice into butter mixture.
5. Gently pour batter into pan over oranges. Bake for 40 to 45 minutes.
6. Turn cake out upside down onto flat surface. Top with orange zest.

APPLE CINNAMON CRISP RICE TREATS

This is a fruity shake-up to the standard crisp rice treat; it is as if bits of apple pie were thrown inside. Think of it as two classic desserts in one!

Makes about 9 bars

1 apple, quartered

1 tablespoon firmly packed light brown sugar

1/2 cup (1 stick) butter, melted

1 teaspoon ground cinnamon

7 cups mini marshmallows, divided

6 cups crisp rice cereal

1. Preheat oven to 400 degrees.
2. Place apple on baking sheet and sprinkle with brown sugar. Roast for 50 minutes.
3. Puree roasted apple in a food processor with butter and cinnamon.
4. Mix warm apple puree with 5 cups mini marshmallows. Stir together until marshmallows are melted.
5. Stir in cereal and 2 cups of mini marshmallows.
6. Press into 9 x 9-inch baking pan and allow to cool.

NANNY'S RICE PUDDING

Making Nanny's Rice Pudding was a bit of a rite of passage for me when I married a Schultz son. Nanny's perfect recipe for my husband's favorite childhood treat requires 45 minutes of nearly constant stirring! The results are absolutely worth it, but if you do not consider stirring a pudding for that length of time feasible, you might call on some sous chefs to take turns.

Serves 4

8 cups milk

1 cup white rice

2/3 cup sugar

1 teaspoon salt

1 tablespoon butter

2 teaspoons vanilla extract

1/4 cup cinnamon sugar (make your own with a 5:1 sugar to cinnamon ratio)

1. Bring the milk, white rice, sugar, salt, and butter to a low boil over medium-high heat in a large saucepan.
2. Reduce heat to medium and stir frequently (about every 30 seconds) for 45 minutes. Remove from heat.
3. Stir in vanilla. Allow to cool. Top with cinnamon sugar.

Happy to Help: A Tip from My Friend

MAKING USE OF MISTAKE FUDGE

Making fudge can be very intimidating. After one terribly disastrous attempt, I hung up my candy thermometer and resigned to simply never become a fudge maker. It was not until my friend Greta came along that I was willing to give it another go. Her family's generations-old recipe for peanut butter fudge is positively unrivaled.

With that sensitive boiling time—and without your own personal Greta in your kitchen—preparing fudge might still bring you some apprehension. Rock-hard or entirely shapeless fudge can foil even the best-laid treat plans. But despair not! Greta even has solutions for mistake fudge: "Fudge that is too soft can be rolled into balls and dipped in melted chocolate for the perfect truffle. And if it is too hard, the fudge can be broken apart in bite-size pieces and sprinkled over ice cream."

If you are keeping track, that is a total of three fine desserts this one recipe can produce. It really is a no-fail recipe.

GRETA'S PEANUT BUTTER FUDGE

I am entirely obsessed with Greta's fudge. When she brings me a batch, I have to force myself to eat only a little at a time (but I am often unsuccessful). You can store this fudge in the freezer, and it is just as delicious and soft when it is frozen.

Makes about 30 pieces

2 pounds (4 2/3 cups) light brown sugar

12 ounces evaporated milk

4 tablespoons light corn syrup

1/4 teaspoon salt

1 cup peanut butter

4 tablespoons (1/2 stick) butter

2 teaspoons vanilla extract

1/2 cup marshmallow crème

1. In large saucepan bring the brown sugar, evaporated milk, corn syrup, and salt to boil over high heat, stirring constantly. Once at a rolling boil, continue to stir for about 4 minutes, or until a candy thermometer reads 235 degrees. Remove from heat and continue to stir for 2 to 3 minutes.

2. Add the peanut butter, butter, vanilla, and marshmallow crème. Continue to stir until smooth.

3. Pour into a greased 9 x 13-inch baking dish. Allow to cool for 1 hour.

WHITE CHOCOLATE TWICE-BAKED SWEET POTATOES

Sweet potatoes are a fun backdrop for a new way to enjoy the classic flavors of a white chocolate macadamia nut cookie. This treat is a little more on the healthy side as far as desserts go, but still completely delicious.

Serves 4

4 sweet potatoes

1/3 cup firmly packed light brown sugar

1/2 teaspoon ground cinnamon

1/4 teaspoon ground nutmeg

1/4 teaspoon salt

3 tablespoons butter

1/2 cup white chocolate chips

1/4 cup macadamia nuts

2 teaspoons honey

1. Preheat oven to 400 degrees.
2. Poke holes into sweet potatoes with fork and bake for 50 minutes. Slice in two lengthwise and allow to cool.
3. Spoon out inside of potatoes and combine with the brown sugar, cinnamon, nutmeg, salt, and butter with an electric mixer on medium-low speed for 1 to 2 minutes.
4. Spoon filling back into potatoes and bake for 15 more minutes.
5. Place white chocolate chips in a microwavable bowl. Microwave on low until smooth, pausing to stir every 30 seconds.
6. Top potatoes with macadamia nuts and drizzle with honey and melted white chocolate.

COCONUT MACAROONS

When I grow tired of regular cookies, I spring for a macaroon. It is different enough to break the boredom, but can still cure any sweet craving. Anytime I am going to a Christmas party, I bring these as a unique alternative to all the other cookies.

Makes 36 macaroons

4 ½ cups sweetened shredded coconut

14 ounces sweetened condensed milk

1 teaspoon vanilla extract

½ teaspoon salt

3 large egg whites

²/₃ cup chocolate chips

1. Preheat oven to 350 degrees.
2. In a bowl combine coconut, sweetened condensed milk, vanilla, and salt.
3. With an electric mixer, whisk egg whites on high for 3 to 4 minutes, until stiffened. Gently fold egg whites into coconut mixture.
4. Shape into 1-inch mounds and arrange on a parchment paper-lined baking sheet.
5. Bake for 14 to 16 minutes.
6. Place chocolate chips in a microwavable bowl. Microwave on low until smooth, pausing to stir every 30 seconds. Drizzle chocolate on cooled macaroons.

S'MORE CUPCAKES

Much of my summer months are spent in hot pursuit of my next s'more. Once Old Man Winter blows in, these cupcake treats are in charge of tiding me over until June's first bonfire.

Makes 24 cupcakes

½ cup (1 stick) butter, softened

½ cup sugar

½ cup firmly packed light brown sugar

1 large egg

1 ¾ cups all-purpose flour

¾ teaspoon baking powder

½ teaspoon salt

1 teaspoon ground cinnamon

1 teaspoon baking soda

½ cup graham cracker crumbs

1 ¾ cups milk

1 cup marshmallow crème

Chocolate Frosting (recipe on page 218)

1. Preheat oven to 350 degrees.
2. In a large bowl stir together the butter, sugar, brown sugar, and egg.
3. In a separate bowl mix the flour, baking powder, salt, cinnamon, baking soda, and graham cracker crumbs. Slowly incorporate milk and flour mixture into butter mixture.
4. Divide batter into a paper cup-lined muffin pan, filling each cup about 2/3 full. Bake for 20 minutes.
5. Using a piping tube, fill cooled cupcakes with marshmallow crème. Top with chocolate frosting.

COCOA AND ZUCCHINI STRAWBERRY SHORTCAKE

For a lighter dessert, I love combining whipped topping and fruit with a quick bread that acts as a shortcake. It's a little bit healthier way to satisfy the sweet tooth.

Serves 20

2 cups all-purpose flour

1/2 cup whole wheat flour

1/2 cup cocoa powder

2 teaspoons baking soda

1/2 teaspoon salt

1 teaspoon ground cinnamon

4 zucchinis, grated (about 2 to 3 cups)

2 large eggs

1 1/2 cups sugar

1/4 cup applesauce

1/2 cup (1 stick) butter, melted

1 teaspoon vanilla extract

16 ounces whipped topping

2 pounds strawberries, sliced

2 cups sweetened shredded coconut

1. Preheat oven to 350 degrees.
2. Combine the all-purpose flour, wheat flour, cocoa, baking soda, salt, and cinnamon in a large bowl.
3. In a separate bowl stir together zucchinis, eggs, sugar, applesauce, butter, and vanilla. Incorporate zucchini mixture into flour mixture.
4. Grease two 9 x 5-inch loaf pans and divide batter between them. Bake for 55 minutes.
5. Slice bread and top with whipped topping, strawberries, and coconut.

BANANA CAKE

It still catches me off guard when I hear people say they do not like chocolate, but these people exist and need desserts too. This is fun for friends who are not fans of the choco-stuff.

Serves 12

1 cup (2 sticks) butter, softened

1 cup firmly packed light brown sugar

3 large eggs

3 very ripe bananas

1 teaspoon vanilla extract

2 1/2 cups all-purpose flour

1 teaspoon baking soda

1 teaspoon baking powder

1/2 teaspoon salt

1 1/2 cups milk

Peanut Butter Frosting (recipe on page 222)

1. Preheat oven to 350 degrees.
2. With an electric mixer combine the butter, brown sugar, eggs, bananas, and vanilla on medium-low speed for 1 to 2 minutes.
3. In a separate bowl stir together the flour, baking soda, baking powder, and salt. Incorporate flour mixture into butter mixture. Stir in milk.
4. Pour batter into a greased 9 x 13-inch baking dish. Bake for 45 to 50 minutes.
5. Allow to cool. Frost with peanut butter frosting.

DOUGHNUT MILKSHAKE

The words doughnut and milkshake together are almost too good to be true. We are devoted doughnut lovers, so it was inevitable that we would put them into more dessert forms. Make enough of these milkshakes to share because a line of people will probably form.

Makes 2 to 3 milkshakes

6 chocolate doughnut holes

2 cups chocolate ice cream

1/2 cup milk

Pinch of salt

Whipped topping

Pinch of cocoa powder

1. Place the doughnut holes, chocolate ice cream, milk, and salt into a blender. Pulse to combine.
2. Pour into glasses and top with whipped topping and a sprinkle of cocoa powder.

STRAWBERRY LEMON SORBET

You might think of sorbet as a difficult dessert to prepare, but it is not! You only need four ingredients to make a faster and healthier ice cream substitute at home.

Makes about 2 pints

3/4 cup water

3/4 cup sugar

4 cups strawberries, frozen

3/4 cup lemon juice

1. In a pot over medium heat, heat 3/4 cup of water and sugar until sugar is dissolved.
2. Combine the sugar water in a blender with strawberries and lemon juice. Blend until smooth.
3. Pour into a loaf pan and freeze for about 4 hours.

Happy to Help: A Tip from My Friend
CLEANING WITH CHILDREN

One way to sum up my friend Danielle might be *confident humility*. Part of that comes from the intelligent, thoughtful personality God blessed her with, but surely much of it comes from the refined-by-fire nature of parenting her seven children (and one on the way).

She is quite inventive in shepherding those little hearts in all things, but also in keeping up with the practical parts of making her home lovely. When preparing her time-tested No-Bake Cookies recipe, she even manages to get the kids to help with cleaning!

Her best tip for this is what she calls "The Bee Game"—a creative way to blur the line between work and play. Everyone must buzz around like a bumblebee, gathering dishes and crumbs as "pollen" before they may harvest the "honey" on the counter (cookies!). As she puts it, "Only after the hive is in order do the bees get their reward and, of course, they share with the queen." This just might be the most adorable and useful game of all time.

DANIELLE'S NO-BAKE COOKIES

Danielle has been perfecting this recipe since she was eight years old. With all that practice, she can now make these in no time flat. That is always helpful when people are calling for some emergency post-dinner dessert.

Makes 30 cookies

½ cup (1 stick) butter

2 ounces cocoa powder

½ cup milk

2 cups sugar

2 teaspoons vanilla extract

³/₄ cup peanut butter

3 cups old-fashioned oats

1. In a medium saucepan over medium heat, melt together the butter, cocoa, and milk. Stir in sugar until dissolved. Increase heat to medium-high and bring to a boil, stirring frequently.
2. Once the mixture begins to bubble, stir constantly until reaching a full, rolling boil. Let boil for 45 seconds. Remove from heat.
3. Stir in the vanilla and peanut butter until melted. Add oats.
4. Scoop into balls and arrange on parchment paper. Allow to set for 15 minutes.

CHOCOLATE FROSTING

Every home baker has to find a good, classic chocolate frosting to have up her sleeve. Just about anything is improved by putting chocolate frosting on it!

Makes about 2 cups

1 cup (2 sticks) butter, softened

2 1/2 cups powdered sugar

1/2 cup cocoa powder

2 tablespoons milk

1/4 teaspoon salt

1 teaspoon vanilla extract

1. Beat butter with an electric mixer on medium speed for 2 minutes.
2. Slowly incorporate powdered sugar.
3. Mix in cocoa, milk, salt, and vanilla until incorporated.

VANILLA FROSTING

Mastering this buttercream is what began my love for making frostings. People always give compliments when I make it for birthdays. It might even outshine the cake.

Makes about 2 cups

1 cup (2 sticks) butter, softened

2 1/2 cups powdered sugar

2 tablespoons milk

1/4 teaspoon salt

1 teaspoon vanilla extract

1. Beat butter with an electric mixer on medium speed for 2 minutes.
2. Slowly incorporate powdered sugar.
3. Mix in milk, salt, and vanilla until incorporated.

PEANUT BUTTER FROSTING

Peanut butter is a really fun flavor to have in frosting form. Of course it would be fabulous with a standard chocolate cupcake, but imagine inventing a PB&J in cupcake form! I use it with Banana Cake on page 210.

Makes about 2 cups

1 cup (2 sticks) butter, softened

1/2 cup peanut butter

2 1/2 cups powdered sugar

2 tablespoons milk

1/4 teaspoon salt

1 teaspoon vanilla extract

1. Beat butter with an electric mixer on medium speed for 2 minutes.
2. Add peanut butter and beat for 1 more minute.
3. Slowly incorporate powdered sugar.
4. Mix in milk, salt, and vanilla until incorporated.

STRAWBERRY FROSTING

*Summer strawberries and homemade jams just beg to be eaten on a
perfect evening in late July. One way you could put a sweet jam to use
would be mixing it into this recipe for a pleasantly pink frosting.*

Makes about 2 cups

1 cup (2 sticks) butter, softened

2 1/2 cups powdered sugar

2 tablespoons milk

1/4 teaspoon salt

1/2 cup strawberry preserves

1 teaspoon vanilla extract

1. Beat butter with an electric mixer on medium speed for 2 minutes.
2. Slowly incorporate powdered sugar.
3. Mix in milk, salt, strawberry preserves, and vanilla until incorporated.

CREAM CHEESE FROSTING

I never used to be a fan of regular cream cheese. Then I tasted cream cheese frosting, which ruined me on the plain stuff even more. It is hard to go back once you have tasted a version so fluffy and sweet!

Makes about 2 cups

1 cup (2 sticks) butter, softened

1 (8-ounce) package cream cheese, softened

2 1/2 cups powdered sugar

2 tablespoons milk

1/4 teaspoon salt

1. Beat butter with an electric mixer on medium speed for 2 minutes.
2. Add cream cheese and beat for 1 more minute.
3. Slowly incorporate powdered sugar.
4. Mix in milk and salt.

PEPPERMINT FROSTING

This frosting is quintessential Christmas. I channel my inner Sugar Plum Fairy the entire time I am making (or eating) it. Spread it across all your December desserts.

Makes about 2 cups

1 cup (2 sticks) butter, softened

2 1/2 cups powdered sugar

2 tablespoons milk

1/4 teaspoon salt

1 teaspoon peppermint extract

1/2 cup peppermint hard candies, crushed

1. Beat butter with an electric mixer on medium speed for 2 minutes.
2. Slowly incorporate powdered sugar.
3. Mix in milk, salt, and peppermint extract until incorporated.
4. Fold in crushed peppermints or sprinkle on top after frosting cake.

NEAPOLITAN SMOOTHIE

This is a yummy drink version of the ice cream classic. Now you can simply position your straw and choose your flavor.

Serves 2

4 cups milk, divided

3 cups strawberries, frozen

1 teaspoon vanilla extract

2/3 cup vanilla yogurt

1 tablespoon honey

1/2 cup chocolate hazelnut spread

3 cups sliced bananas, frozen

Mint leaves

1. In advance, pour 2 1/2 cups milk into ice cube trays and freeze.
2. To make the strawberry layer, combine strawberries and 1 1/4 cups milk in blender until smooth. Set aside and rinse blender.
3. For the vanilla layer, combine vanilla, milk ice cubes, yogurt, and honey in blender until smooth. Set aside and rinse blender.
4. For the chocolate layer, combine chocolate hazelnut spread, bananas, and 1/4 cup milk.
5. Layer the strawberry, vanilla, and chocolate into two drinking glasses. Garnish with mint.

SUGAR-ROASTED SLOW COOKER ALMONDS

People are always impressed with this easy, slow-cooked treat. These almonds can also make a sweet, inexpensive Christmas gift for friends. They look adorable wrapped in butcher-paper cones or stored in jars tied with a festive ribbon.

Makes 3 cups

1 cup sugar

1 cup firmly packed light brown sugar

2 tablespoons ground cinnamon

A dash of salt

1 large egg white

2 teaspoons vanilla extract

3 cups almonds

1/4 cup water

1. Stir together the sugar, brown sugar, cinnamon, and salt in a slow cooker.
2. In a separate bowl whisk egg white with vanilla. Add almonds and stir until all almonds are coated with egg mixture.
3. Pour almonds into slow cooker and stir with sugar mixture.
4. Cook on high for 2 hours, stirring every 30 minutes.
5. When 30 minutes of cook time remains, add 1/4 cup of water to slow cooker and stir.
6. Transfer almonds onto parchment paper over a flat surface to cool.

INDEX

LIST OF GLUTEN-FREE RECIPES

Spinach and Mushroom Polenta

Three Cheese Omelet

Flourless Yogurt and Banana Pancakes

Pumpkin and Pecan Baked Oatmeal

Maple Sweet Potato Hash Browns

Apple Cookies

Avocado Deviled Eggs

Vanessa's Sweet Potato and Asparagus Salad

Loaded Skillet Fries

Watermelon and Pistachio Salad

Coconut Almond Chocolate Popcorn

Almond and Pear Baked Brie (serve with
gluten-free bread or crackers)

Blueberry Cheese Ball (serve with gluten-
free bread or crackers)

Raspberry Roasted Cheese Dip (serve with
gluten-free bread or crackers)

Spaghetti Squash Burrito Bowls

Hawaiian Slow Cooker Chicken (substitute
gluten-free teriyaki sauce)

Southwestern Stuffed Peppers

Apple Cider Beef Stew (serve without bread
or with gluten-free bread)

Jenny's Mushroom Braciole

Chicken Fried Rice (substitute gluten-free
soy sauce)

Chicken Tortilla Soup (with corn-based
tortilla chips)

Balsamic Pesto Chicken with Quinoa

Spaghetti Squash Pad Thai (substitute gluten-
free soy sauce)

Shepherd's Pie Cakes

Brad's Spatchcock Chicken

Plum Caprese Stuffed Pork Loin

Loaded Baked Potato Gnocchi

Raspberry Basil Whipped Butter

Walnut Pesto

Blue Cheese Sauce

Apple and Parmesan Coleslaw

Pomegranate Wheat Berry Salad (substitute
quinoa or rice)

Bethany's Blanched Vegetable Medley

Roasted Asparagus

Greek Seasoning

Mexican Seasoning

Italian Seasoning

Cajun Seasoning

Salsa

Roasted Vegetable Guacamole

Grandma's Cucumber Salad

Carrot and Parsnip Fries

Mashed Potato Casserole

Coconut Lemon Bars

Nanny's Rice Pudding

Greta's Peanut Butter Fudge

White Chocolate Twice-Baked Sweet
Potatoes

Coconut Macaroons

Strawberry Lemon Sorbet

Danielle's No-Bake Cookies

Chocolate Frosting

Vanilla Frosting

Peanut Butter Frosting

Strawberry Frosting

Cream Cheese Frosting

Peppermint Frosting

Neapolitan Smoothie

Sugar-Roasted Slow Cooker Almonds

ACKNOWLEDGMENTS

I have been blessed by my local church in more ways than I can count. Thank you first to my elders and pastors who carefully shepherd my family and me.

Andrew Wolgemuth, they were right; you really are the best agent in the business.

Molly Hodgin, Carrie Marrs, and Laura Minchew, thank you for pursuing me and seeing this project through. It has been a treat.

Natalie Minnaar, your sweet spirit and hard work were a great help to me in this process. I would not have wanted to do it without you! Our family loves you.

Kevin DeYoung, it has been a frightening privilege to have my work go under the wrath of your red pen. Thank you for your guidance and availability.

To the friends who shared contributions, your pieces gave the book added variety, spice, and wisdom. Thank you, Brad Beals, Bethany Ehrlich, Stefan Hull, Carolyn Isenga, Greta Lankheet, Carissa Minnaar, Vanessa Saunders, Niki Shirkman, Danielle Spencer, and Jenny Vanderwey.

Many recipe testers helped edit this book. Thank you, Evelyn Schumacher, Jen Lane, Jordan Ng, Katie Clifford, Cheri Martin, Robin Ricica, Karen Zeilstra, Matt Bushart, Sue Seymour, Simeon Lowe, Austin Wilson, Jamie Dilworth, Dinah Schultz, Brittany Viscomi, Carri Eisenbeis, Emily Zuiderveen, Amie Ehnis, Nicole Johnson, Dana Rodriguez, Lindsey Immelman, Jamie Schultz, Erik Wolgemuth, Ani Vanderwey, Susan Kreider, Paul Beard, Vikki Dipple, Kim Dickinson-Lukins, Vanessa Chesebro, and Victoria Young.

David Schultz, it is all for you.

ABOUT THE AUTHOR

Rachel Schultz is an author, podcast host, and dessert activist. A few of her favorite things are cake, Nutella, bubble baths, *The Lord of the Rings*, the smell of coffee, her husband, going to church, books, chocolate-covered pretzels, yogurt-covered pretzels, basically anything-covered pretzels, and cake again. Her food and home decor lifestyle blog has been read internationally by millions, but mainly she is just an ordinary homemaker living in Michigan with her husband, David, and their two children.